BUDDHISM IN A NEW LIGHT

BUDDHISM IN A NEW LIGHT

Eighteen Essays That Illuminate
Our Buddhist Practice

SHIN YATOMI

Published by World Tribune Press
606 Wilshire Blvd.
Santa Monica, CA 90401

© 2006 SGI-USA

ISBN-13: 978-1-932911-14-5
ISBN-10: 1-932911-14-6

Design by Gopa & Ted2, Inc.

10 9 8 7 6 5 4 3

Table of Contents

Editor's Note

IN 1991, the Nichiren Shoshu priesthood excommunicated SGI members worldwide. In response, the SGI turned to the basics of Buddhist practice, including the study of Nichiren Daishonin's writings and the fundamentals of Buddhism. Simultaneously, care and compassion for each person became the renewed focus of the SGI. All this served to clarify the critical importance of understanding the human issues that led to this situation.

In the following essays, Shin Yatomi, SGI-USA Study Department leader, delves into topics such as the meaning of freedom and the difference between arrogance and confidence, in effect revealing a fresh perspective in understanding Nichiren Buddhism. The SGI-USA Soka Spirit Committee worked closely in support of this project.

"Introduction" was first published on the SGI-USA's Web site (www.sokaspirit.org) in March 2003. Chapters 1 through 15 originally appeared in the *World Tribune* between September 2001 and January 2005. Chapter 16 originally appeared in the February 2002 *Living Buddhism*; Chapter 17 in the February 2005 *Living Buddhism*; and Chapter 18 in the

September 2005 *Living Buddhism*. They are collected in this volume with minor editorial changes.

These essays are offered with the hope that they may assist the practitioners of Nichiren Buddhism in clarifying the meaning of faith and practice as intended by Nichiren Daishonin.

The following abbreviations appear in some citations:

✦ WND, page number(s)—refers to *The Writings of Nichiren Daishonin* (Tokyo: Soka Gakkai, 1999)

✦ GZ, page number(s)—refers to *Nichiren Daishonin Gosho Zenshu* [The Complete Writings of Nichiren Daishonin; the Japanese-language compilation of Nichiren's writings] (Tokyo: Soka Gakkai, 1952)

✦ OTT, page number(s)—refers to *The Record of the Orally Transmitted Teachings* [the compilation of Nichiren's oral teachings on the Lotus Sutra], translated by Burton Watson (Tokyo: Soka Gakkai, 2004)

✦ LS, page number(s)—refers to *The Lotus Sutra*, translated by Burton Watson (New York: Columbia University Press, 1993)

Compassion To Care, Courage To Challenge

THE SOKA SPIRIT is the essential spirit of Buddhism to promote humanism and stem authoritarianism—the Japanese word *soka* signifying the creation of value. It is based on fundamental respect for the universal dignity and equality of life as expounded in the Lotus Sutra, a scripture of Mahayana Buddhism. The Soka Spirit is expressed in the joint workings of the compassion to care for life and the courage to challenge disrespect toward life.

This essential spirit of Buddhism was exemplified by Nichiren Daishonin, a Buddhist reformer in thirteenth-century Japan, who was most concerned about the plight of the suffering while challenging corrupt religious and political authority at the risk of his life. It has also been the spirit advocated and practiced by the three founding presidents of the Soka Gakkai—Tsunesaburo Makiguchi, Josei Toda and Daisaku Ikeda.

We in the SGI-USA are striving to embody the Soka Spirit through our individual and collective efforts to understand and practice Nichiren Buddhism while challenging that which opposes the equality of and respect for human beings.

The SGI-USA's advocacy of the Soka Spirit is a historic movement to restore the original meaning of Buddhism, or religion itself, as an internal guide to happiness rather than an external authority that subjugates human decency to its dogma. Through our example, furthermore, we hope to inspire the transformation of religion from a cause of violence and intolerance into a catalyst for peace and equality.

Three Ways the Soka Spirit Matters to Our Lives

1) THE SOKA SPIRIT MATTERS TO THE SURVIVAL OF BUDDHISM

As flowing water keeps itself pure, any stream of thought or religion seeking to purify human life must continually clarify and reaffirm its purpose. This is particularly true of Buddhism, which teaches the universality of Buddhahood, the supreme essence of human life common to all people.

The Soka Spirit refers to this forward momentum of self-purification. Such purification comes from keeping the humane and empowering essence of Buddhism flowing like a clear stream from one person's life to another. It is also enhanced by educating others and ourselves about the importance of guarding this stream against pollution. Such pollution arises from base, self-centered human inclinations, such as greed, anger and foolishness concerning the true value and dignity of life. These are known in Buddhism as the three poisons.

The Soka Spirit means to be diligent in winning over

these base proclivities in us. It also means recognizing and standing up against them when they appear in the actions of others. These two aspects of the Soka Spirit support each other: Challenging negativity in ourselves enables us to recognize and stand up to it when it takes hold of others. Challenging destructive impulses in others helps us to recognize and overcome the selfsame potential in ourselves.

Those who wish to spread positive ideals and values have to organize their efforts in order to do so effectively. With organization, however, comes the potential for corruption and authoritarianism. The Soka Spirit is a potent antidote to protect the humane essence of Buddhism from the potential poisons of self-interest that may creep into any institution formed to uphold and spread religious teachings. The integrity and survival of Buddhism, therefore, depend upon the Soka Spirit.

2) THE SOKA SPIRIT MATTERS TO OUR HAPPINESS

Nichiren Daishonin teaches that our lives are originally endowed with the potential for both enlightenment and delusion. Enlightenment is the realization of life's supreme potential, and delusion its negation. The true benefit of our Buddhist practice lies in our consistent efforts to nurture enlightenment and stem delusion.

To strengthen our innate enlightenment, we must develop the compassion to care for life by recognizing Buddhahood in others and ourselves. To stem our innate delusion, we must develop the courage to challenge our inclination to disrespect life while helping others do the same. Through our understanding of the Soka Spirit, we can continue to develop such compassion and courage, as they are indispensable to our genuine happiness.

3) THE SOKA SPIRIT MATTERS TO OUR FUTURE

War is the cause of much of humanity's suffering, and the abuse of religion is the cause of many wars. To eliminate war and establish lasting peace, people must stop the abuse of religion as a pretext for war. Indeed, religious passion that leads to violence and revenge is the greatest offense to religion itself since the fundamental purpose of religion is people's happiness and well-being.

One cause for the abuse of religion may be the prevalent view of religion as an external authority. When people view religious truth as superior and human beings as subordinate to that truth, then universal human values—such as respect for life, human equality and empathy for others—become secondary and are easily compromised.

Through the Soka Spirit movement, the SGI-USA is striving to establish a clear understanding that the fundamental purpose of religion is people's happiness and well-being. We are doing this by sharing the humanistic ideals and practice of Nichiren Buddhism with as many people as possible. It is the conviction of the SGI that religion should exist to serve the ordinary people; they do not exist to serve religion or religious authority. While challenging any authoritarian or discriminatory interpretation of Nichiren Buddhism and reconfirming its universal humanism, the SGI-USA hopes to stand as an example of this empowering spirit to create a peaceful world in which no human life is debased in the name of religion and the paramount concern of religious leaders is nothing other than human happiness.

The Priesthood Issue and the Soka Spirit

Today, the principles of the Soka Spirit are being applied in the SGI-USA's current efforts to counter the distortions of Nichiren Buddhism propounded by Nichiren Shoshu, a school of Nichiren Buddhism based in Shizuoka, Japan, with six branch temples in the United States. Nichiren Shoshu is the Buddhist school with which the Soka Gakkai and the SGI were originally affiliated. Under the leadership of its 67th high priest, Nikken Abe, however, Nichiren Shoshu committed two major transgressions against Buddhism and its practitioners.

In 1991, the Nichiren Shoshu priesthood demanded that the Soka Gakkai, then its lay organization, be disbanded and later officially excommunicated it. Buddhism describes disrupting the harmony among believers as one of the most serious offenses in Buddhism. Furthermore, in an attempt to justify its arbitrary action toward the SGI and to silence believers' criticism, the priesthood has propounded the erroneous doctrine of "absolute faith in and strict obedience to the High Priest" (*Dai-Nichiren*, Special Edition II, "The Correct Way of Faith in Nichiren Shoshu," published by the Nichiren Shoshu Bureau of Religious Affairs, p. 13).

Because the priesthood has used its assumed authority and role as clergy to condemn the SGI and actively aims to confound and intimidate believers, the SGI has seen the urgent necessity to address the issue. In addition, addressing and correcting such abuse by religious authority accord exactly with the teachings and spirit of Buddhism. Beyond these specific issues, however, we consider the priesthood issue an excellent opportunity to deepen our understanding of the Soka Spirit and reflect upon ourselves and the future of our movement to spread Nichiren Buddhism.

The priesthood issue is an experience of historic importance from which future generations of Buddhists will learn how to apply the core spirit of Buddhism to their changing circumstances.

The Soka Spirit Is for Everyone

The Soka Spirit informs the three basic aspects of Nichiren Buddhism—faith, practice and study—with the humanistic essence of Buddhism. A certain religious teaching eventually may be interpreted and practiced differently by various individuals or groups. In this regard, the perspective from which one views religion and the approach with which one practices it are as important as the teaching itself.

For instance, whether one believes that religion exists to

serve people or that people exist to serve religion will make a great difference in how one views a religion's doctrines or scriptures. The question of whether the ultimate truth or reality is intrinsic to human life or is external to and above human life is also a key. The importance of our perspective on and approach to religion becomes most evident when we see in today's world the same religions being practiced by both violent fundamentalists and peace-loving ordinary citizens.

The Soka Spirit may be described as the authentically Buddhist perspective on the belief, practice and learning of Buddhism. It reflects the conviction that all living beings equally share the potential for supreme enlightenment. It views Buddhism as existing to empower all people equally—regardless of race, nationality, sex, social class or position—to develop the highest form of wisdom and genuine fulfillment in their lives. The following are four ways in which the Soka Spirit informs how we believe, practice and learn about Nichiren Buddhism.

1) PRAYER: PRAISING AND REFLECTING UPON OUR TRUE SELF

Prayer is an expression of faith. The content of prayer, therefore, is the substance of faith. The prayer of authoritarian faith is the prayer of self-disparagement, whereas the prayer of humanistic faith is the prayer of self-affirmation. Prayer based on the Soka Spirit is the total affirmation of one's true self, which is originally endowed with fundamental enlightenment and delusion; it is the expression of one's resolve to nurture our enlightenment and challenge our delusion. In this regard, we may say that, through prayer, we praise our lives for our innate Buddhahood and self-reflect upon our delusive tendency to disrespect life.

Our acknowledgment of both our innate enlightenment and innate delusion is a cause for great joy. From steadfast confidence in our innate Buddhahood, we can create hope in any circumstance; we can tap the life force and wisdom that can contribute to the improvement of ourselves and our circumstances. A courageous and honest recognition of our innate potential for delusion can inspire us to continually improve our lives. Through praising our innate enlightenment and reflecting upon our innate delusion, we can live today with confidence and appreciation and look with hope toward tomorrow. Practicing Buddhism with this spirit, we can come to know our true selves.

2) LEARNING: KNOWING GOOD AND EVIL WITHIN

The Soka Spirit inspires people to learn the Buddhist view of human life—of both its good and evil sides. From the viewpoint of Buddhism, good is the affirmation of life, particularly its supreme potential of Buddhahood, and evil is its negation. The innate good of life expresses itself as humanism, that is, a respectful orientation toward life that regards fulfilling life's highest potential as most important. Life's innate evil, however, manifests as a disrespectful view that life is a means to an end.

The vast literature of Buddhism, particularly the Lotus Sutra and Nichiren's writings, sheds light on the workings of life and explains how to nurture our innate good while challenging our innate evil. Reading about and discussing the priesthood issue, as a concrete example of these workings of life, will give us important insight into the causes of authoritarianism and the importance of the Soka Spirit. Learning about the humanistic essence of Buddhism is to gain intimate knowledge of our true self.

3) DIALOGUE: TALKING THE SOKA SPIRIT

The Soka Spirit deepens and spreads through dialogue. When we share our thoughts and feelings about it with others, we not only help them expand their perspective on life but also deepen our own understanding. When imbued with the compassion to care for others and the courage to challenge disrespect toward life, dialogue is a concrete and powerful expression of the Soka Spirit, whether or not we specifically mention the SGI or Buddhism.

The possibilities of the practical application of the Soka Spirit are limitless and as diverse as our human activities. The Soka Spirit could permeate every dialogue—from peace talks among world leaders to dinner-table conversations. We can make the Soka Spirit the foundation of our everyday communication and share the message of compassion and courage with our families and friends.

4) ACTION: WALKING THE SOKA SPIRIT

An idea becomes reality when put into action. If people wish to appreciate the meaning and value of the Soka Spirit, they need to practice it every day in the form of respectful actions toward others and themselves. When we praise our lives through strong Buddhist prayer and treat others with respect, when we reflect upon our disrespect of others and ourselves, and when we encourage others to challenge their delusion, we are on the path of the Soka Spirit. It is a path that becomes more distinct as we keep walking.

Respect for life is the fundamental teaching of Buddhism, and the Lotus Sutra explains its importance through the example of Bodhisattva Never Disparaging. If we take an honest look at how we treat ourselves and others, and if we try to be a little more respectful and a little less disrespectful, we become practitioners of the Soka Spirit.

It takes mindfulness and perseverance to practice the Soka Spirit, since all people may not reciprocate our respect. As an example of this attitude in the Lotus Sutra, Bodhisattva Never Disparaging, though reviled and disparaged, continued to show respect for all people while praising their potential for Buddhahood.

As the Lotus Sutra teaches, each step we take along the path of the Soka Spirit will be richly rewarding, enabling us to deepen our character and sense of fulfillment. The Lotus Sutra explains that Bodhisattva Never Disparaging, as a result of his respect for others, purified his mind and senses, that is, his thoughts and feelings. When we start embracing those around us with the Soka Spirit, we will purify our mind and senses, just as Bodhisattva Never Disparaging did, experiencing our lives anew each day.

> (from the SGI-USA's Soka Spirit Web site,
> www.sokaspirit.org, March 2003)

Key Points for Chapter 1

1) Through understanding the priesthood issue, we can clarify the meaning of our faith and experience greater joy and benefit from our Buddhist practice.

2) Those who follow the priesthood's teaching say that they believe in the Gohonzon, yet the way they view the Gohonzon is the exact opposite of what Nichiren Daishonin teaches. Specifically, the priesthood separates the object of devotion from our inherent Buddha nature.

3) Genuine faith in the Gohonzon is to develop confidence in the unconditional value of our lives. As Nichiren Daishonin encourages us: "You, yourself, are a Thus Come One who is originally enlightened and endowed with the three bodies [of a Buddha]. You should chant Nam-myoho-renge-kyo with this conviction" (WND, 299–300).

CHAPTER 1

The "Problem" of Faith

THE SOKA SPIRIT movement is a gold mine of opportunities to learn more about Nichiren Buddhism. The basics of faith are now cast in new light, revealing their deeper meaning in contrast with the Nichiren Shoshu priesthood's erroneous views. For this reason, one's understanding of the Soka Spirit will naturally translate into greater joy and benefit based on a clearer view of faith.

The Meaning of Faith

The meaning of faith, for example, once required a simple explanation, such as belief in the Gohonzon—the object of devotion in Nichiren Buddhism. Many Nichiren Buddhists assumed that it was impossible to have wrong faith in the correct object of devotion. Faith, as long as it was placed in the Gohonzon, was a matter of strong or weak, not of right or wrong, they believed.

Now, thanks to the priesthood, we are learning that what matters is not only what we believe in but also *how* we believe in it, that what people sometimes think of as faith in the Gohonzon can be a problem.

Regarding the significance of the Gohonzon, Nichiren Daishonin states, "Never seek this Gohonzon outside yourself" (WND, 832). Interpreting this passage, the priesthood asserts: "The Gohonzon to which he refers is not the correct object of worship which one should worship. The Gohonzon to which he refers is the life of the Buddha nature endowed within our bodies" (*Refuting the Soka Gakkai's Counterfeit Object of Worship: 100 Questions and Answers*, published by Nichiren Shoshu Temple, p. 56). The priesthood here separates the object of devotion from our inherent Buddha nature; in other words, the Gohonzon to which we pray and the ultimate reality of our lives are two different things, or so the priests say.

The priesthood's view of faith, however, contradicts Nichiren's teaching. As he admonishes us, "When we revere Myoho-renge-kyo inherent in our own life as the object of devotion, the Buddha nature within us is summoned forth and manifested by our chanting of Nam-myoho-renge-kyo" (WND, 887). Those who follow the priesthood's teaching say that they believe in the Gohonzon, yet the way they do is the exact opposite of what Nichiren teaches. The innermost reality of their prayer, whether they are conscious or unconscious of it, is more likely: *The Gohonzon is all-powerful and worthy of respect, but I'm nothing, except inasmuch as I receive blessings through my faith in its power.*

The Meaning of Prayer

Those who pray this way grow dependent, passive and weak; they remain insecure and frustrated because they separate themselves from the solution to their suffering and thus have no control over their existence.

In contrast, genuine faith in the Gohonzon is to develop confidence in the unconditional value of our lives as Nichiren encourages us: "You, yourself, are a Thus Come One who is originally enlightened and endowed with the three bodies [of a Buddha]. You should chant Nam-myoho-renge-kyo with this conviction" (WND, 299–300).

Our faith in and reverence for the Gohonzon, therefore, must be reflected back to ourselves as faith in and reverence for our own life. Our innate Buddha nature is the object of fundamental respect as it is represented in the Gohonzon; it must be recognized, cherished and praised daily through prayer. Any form of self-disparagement, therefore, should have no place in faith or in prayer.

To see our supreme potential and to respect ourselves despite our momentary appearance or the opinions of others are of far greater significance and much more difficult than to humble ourselves before some omnipotent entity. This is why genuine faith requires courage. But every bit of courage we exert to praise our lives will be richly rewarded with hope and freedom.

(from the September 7, 2001, *World Tribune*)

FOOD FOR THOUGHT:

✦ The problem of faith is often the problem of motivation. Do you sometimes pray out of fear and anxiety that you are essentially helpless in your circumstances? What action can you take to change that?

✦ In your prayer, are you begging while disparaging yourself or are you determined to win while praising yourself? What do you think is the meaning of prayer in Nichiren Buddhism?

KEY POINTS FOR CHAPTER 2

1) Authoritarianism results from the deep-seated human weakness to give up oneself to external authority.

2) Violence is a deliberate wish for the destruction of life; it is a symptom of the weak, passive self that seeks to validate its existence by dominating and destroying other lives or things of value to others.

3) One of the most concrete and powerful ways to oppose violence and authoritarianism is prayer that sincerely affirms the power of life—both within our lives and in the lives of others.

CHAPTER 2

Violence Is Weakness, Prayer Is Power

IT IS HARD TO TELL what thoughts were running through the minds of the terrorists as they plunged airplanes into the World Trade Center towers, the Pentagon and a field in western Pennsylvania on September 11, 2001. Judging from their irrational acts, however, it seems that they surrendered their power of reason and human decency to a higher power of their imagination—whether it was their political ideal or God. Such perversion of philosophy and religion occurs when people subordinate the dignity of life to ideology and dogma. Philosophy and religion must serve people and preserve life. As Nichiren Daishonin admonishes, "Life is the foremost of all treasures" (WND, 1125).

What we saw on that day was the destructiveness of the human tendency to give oneself up to external authority. This deep-seated human weakness is called authoritarianism, which many people, if not all, share to some degree. As the September 11 tragedy illustrates, violence is often an outcome of an authoritarian orientation—a willingness to give up our freedom and independence to external authority in exchange for the false, temporary sense of security that may be felt upon our release from the burden of responsibility to seek self-knowledge and shape our own destiny.

The Nature of Violence

Violence is a deliberate wish, expressed or unexpressed in word or deed, for the destruction of life; it is a symptom of the weak, passive self that seeks to validate its existence through dominating and destroying other lives or things valued by others. Violent people are weak, for they cannot find the inner strength to overcome their insecurity or aloneness and, therefore, must destroy others so that they may feel empowered. Their power, however, is an illusion since it is *over* others, not from *within*.

Power derived by subjugating others is merely a fancy because it requires others and is dependent on them. On the other hand, power created from within is genuine because it is independent and free. In other words, power is not real so long as it comes from human weakness or depends on the external.

Despite their aggressive appearance, violent people are passive at the core of their existence because violence is essentially an easy escape from an overwhelming sense of inner powerlessness and isolation, from the responsibility and effort required to make personal change. It is easier to hurt someone else than get real about oneself. A person who resorts to violence as an escape from his or her inner challenge is not the originator of self-willed action and is passive in his or her mental reality. The sense of power felt by violent people, therefore, is actually a sign of their weakness and passivity.

Moreover, the sense of power derived from destructive acts is short-lived and addictive; it can only be sustained through further destruction. Compelled by their inner powerlessness, violent people continue to destroy, and when they find nothing more to destroy or find themselves prevented from further acts of destruction, they destroy themselves to escape from themselves, which are the source of their powerlessness. In this sense, violence is not a reaction to external objects per se but rather a destructive drive arising from inner weakness simply waiting for a convenient outlet.

The Meaning of Self-defense

To better understand the relationship of violence and authoritarianism, it is worthwhile to take a closer look at the ideas of self-defense and sacrifice. Pure self-defense is not violence because it is based solely on the affirmation of life rather than its negation. It has been reported that one of the hijacked airplanes crashed short of its intended target in an unpopulated area of western Pennsylvania, probably because some passengers struggled with the terrorists for control of the airplane. Their action was courageous and noble; it was not violence but self-defense since they were motivated by their desire to protect and preserve life. Quite often, however, so-called self-defense is disguised aggression in which one's real motive for the destruction of life is suppressed consciously or unconsciously by self-deceptive rationalization.

The difference between violence and self-defense lies not merely in the external circumstances, but more significantly in one's true motive. In this regard, Shakyamuni's injunction to "kill the will to kill" reveals profound Buddhist insight into the nature of violence (see *My Dear Friends in America*, p. 129). Behind the passionate emotions or seemingly sound rhetoric of self-defense is often hidden the "will to kill."

Violence arises from a will to harm, and self-defense from a will to protect, although both employ physical force as a means. It is necessary to look inward to see one's true motive—whether it is to preserve life or to harm life. We become capable of self-defense with the ability of self-reflection, to which one of the greatest obstacles is an authoritarian orientation that looks outside for the motive in order to escape responsibility. Authoritarian people are incapable of self-defense, because they have neither a sense of responsibility nor a willingness to self-reflect.

The Two Types of Sacrifice

Sacrifice is often praised as one of the highest virtues, but we witnessed in the September 11 tragedy that there are two kinds of sacrifice. One is motivated by self-denial.

Some people make such a sacrifice because in doing so they can lose themselves to an external power and thus become part of what is not them. They are motivated by a desire to escape from themselves whom they neither love nor trust. Through making such a sacrifice, however, they lose the freedom and integrity to think and act as individuals. This kind of sacrifice is authoritarian in essence, and it is a sign of one's weakness and inability to freely express oneself.

Another type of sacrifice is the complete opposite of self-denial; it is self-expression. Some people courageously choose—instead of being forced by external authority—to sacrifice their physical safety or even their lives as the utmost expression of their spiritual integrity. Their sacrifice is an assertion of individual freedom and will. The line between those two types of sacrifice was drawn clearly in the September 11 terrorist attacks. While the terrorists were giving up their power of critical thinking and, with it, their humanity to external authority, passengers on the hijacked airplanes and those trapped in the collapsing buildings valiantly faced their final moments in efforts to save others and in their prayers for their loved ones.

The terrorists' acts may seem "active," but in their innermost reality they are passive and feeble, while the quiet thoughts and prayers of many who died in the attacks—despite the superficial appearance of helplessness and passivity in the eyes of the terrorists—were the greatest expressions of their will and love. In their final thoughts and prayers, they were strong and free.

Understanding Authoritarianism

As we came face to face with the destructiveness of authoritarianism, what happened on September 11 may serve as an opportunity for us to gain deeper insight into the nature of violence and learn the meaning of freedom from those who made a true sacrifice. As violence stems from the authoritarian character of submission and domination, which is in turn a manifestation of the enfeebled self, any attempt to suppress violence with further violence may only be described as foolishness.

How many times must humanity repeat the same mistake of trying to cure violence with more violence? In this regard, Nichiren Daishonin warns us, "If you try to treat someone's illness without knowing its cause, you will only make the person sicker than before" (WND, 774). This is the time that we must cure this greatest ailment of human civilization at its root. We must seriously think about ways to empower people, not only economically and politically but also spiritually, so that we may limit human destructiveness. Each of us must deeply reflect upon our own authoritarian tendency to give up so easily our freedom and power of reason to external authority.

In one sense, the Soka Spirit movement lies in our efforts to understand the nature of authoritarianism; it is a process in which we develop our ability to both self-reflect and think critically about what is happening in our environment. As we have learned from the Nichiren Shoshu priesthood, even the humanistic teachings of Buddhism can become authoritarian depending upon its practitioners' understanding and action.

This important lesson becomes genuine only when we realize that the absence of a priesthood does not necessarily mean the end of authoritarianism, and that each of us is responsible to understand and practice Buddhism as the humanistic teaching Nichiren intended it to be.

Likewise, although the vast majority of religions in the world are founded upon the principles of love and peace, through the many atrocities and tragedies in history, we have repeatedly been made aware how easily irrational zealots can pervert any religion into authoritarian dogma that enslaves people. More than ever, it is crucial for us to reaffirm our commitment to the humanistic tenets of our beliefs and shun the forces of authoritarianism from within and without.

The Power of Prayer

One of the most concrete and powerful ways to oppose violence and authoritarianism is prayer that sincerely affirms the power of life—both within oneself and in the lives of others. The ideas of nonviolence and humanism can change the way people live when those ideas are both understood intellectually and also felt deeply in their hearts' core. As Gandhi eloquently said: "Let there be no cant about nonviolence. It is not like a garment to be put on and off at will.

Its seat is in the heart, and it must be an inseparable part of our very being" (*Non-Violence in Peace and War,* vol. 1, p. 66). Prayer is our precious tool to discover the dormant dignity of life. As Nichiren states, "Chanting Nam-myoho-renge-kyo is what is meant by entering the palace of oneself" (OTT, 209).

Prayer is a process in which we transform the abstract idea of life's dignity into a concrete reality that is felt in the depths of our lives and with our personal conviction, which is displayed in how we treat with respect both others and ourselves.

Whatever faiths we Americans embrace today, our prayers must be united in our love for life and peace. If we are to hate anything, let us hate hatred and violence with a single heart. From such a united prayer of true strength and patriotism will emerge a new America free of violence. As many people have shown through their courage in the face of the September 11 tragedy, violence is weakness, and prayer is power.

(from the October 5, 2001, World Tribune)

FOOD FOR THOUGHT:

✦ Revenge is an act of violence because its chief motive is to harm rather than preserve life, and it is often used merely as an outlet for irrational emotions. What can each of us do to prevent America and the rest of the world from falling deeper into the cycle of violence and revenge?

✦ Authoritarianism is the abandonment of freedom and integrity to an external authority. Humanism encourages individual freedom and integrity from within. What can each of us do to make our practice of Nichiren Buddhism truly humanistic and prevent future practitioners from falling into authoritarianism?

KEY POINTS FOR CHAPTER 3

1) It is important to recognize the unconditional value of life within us. To enjoy fulfilling lives, we need to stop judging our worth by comparing ourselves with others.

2) Nichiren Daishonin explains our innate Buddhahood as an absolute value of goodness—that is, good in and of itself, not because of external conditions. To awaken to this treasure inside is authentic happiness.

3) One of the greatest ways to praise ourselves is through prayer that sincerely affirms our supreme potential. As we recognize our own Buddhahood, we cannot help but recognize the same quality in others, which further strengthens self-esteem.

CHAPTER 3

The Way We See Ourselves

AN IMPORTANT ASPECT of what we call enlightenment, or human revolution, is to change the way we see ourselves and thus to see the unconditional value of life within us, which neither requires comparison with others nor depends upon our transient appearance. It is a simple idea yet requires a difficult change of perspective since most of us are accustomed to judging ourselves by how well we fulfill socially prescribed roles in comparison with others. Those roles are often related to status or gender but rarely to individual uniqueness.

Judging Oneself Through the Eyes of Others

As early as elementary school or even before, people start learning to judge themselves in terms of others: "I'm not as smart as other kids," or "I'm not as slim as other girls." Later in life, many people continue to judge their worth in the same way: "I'm a loser because I don't make as much money as most successful men do," or "I'm miserable because I'm not married as all happy women should be." With subtle yet repeated reinforcement and censure from society, we learn to live through the eyes of others, to think of our happiness in terms of ideas borrowed from or imposed upon us by others. In America, people are free to express their thoughts, but not many seem to have thoughts or even feelings of their own.

Nichiren Daishonin explains our innate Buddhahood as an absolute value of goodness, often describing it with expressions such as *unmade* (Jpn *musa*), *originally endowed* (Jpn *hon'nu*) or *eternally dwelling* (Jpn *joju*). Buddhahood, in other words, is good in and of itself, not because of external conditions or circumstances. To awaken to this treasure within us is happiness, while our ignorance of it spells suffering. As Nichiren states, "When deluded, one is called an ordinary being, but when enlightened, one is called a Buddha" (WND, 4).

The sad irony of modern men and women who have lost touch with their own lives is echoed in Nichiren's words: "If you seek enlightenment outside yourself, then your performing...even ten thousand good deeds will be in vain. It is like the case of a poor man who spends night and day counting his neighbor's wealth but gains not even half a coin" (WND, 3). All the hard work we do for our success and happiness would be wasted if those ideas were simply imposed on us from the outside and naïvely accepted without critical thinking and reflection.

Deriving self-worth by comparing ourselves with others is one of our most destructive habits. It may even be described as a form of self-inflicted violence since it weakens us by *de*-centering our existence in the sense that it shifts the center of power to decide the meaning of our lives to the outside. We let others decide what our happiness is instead of deciding for ourselves. With the power of self-determination lost to external authority, we are neither free nor independent. Since we live in a competitive society where this sort of comparison is encouraged and often unavoidable, it is a difficult habit to break, but to do so is crucial to our genuine fulfillment and freedom.

It is ironic that the original meaning of the word *compete* derives from the Latin *com*, "together," and *petere*, "to seek" or "to strive." Competition did not originally connote comparison; it meant "to strive together for shared goals." Just as Nichiren characterizes the state of anger as "contention and strife" (WND, 100), competition in society often gives rise to anger, overt or suppressed.

To judge self-worth by comparing oneself with others is essentially an authoritarian way of life in which one seeks comfort and security in the approval of an external power. To unlearn such an authoritarian orientation and build a society in which people may live true to their unique identities is certainly an aspiration of our multifaceted Soka Spirit movement, which aims for the liberation of individuals from all forms of authoritarianism, both within and without.

Awakening to Our Intrinsic Value

One way to overcome our tendency to compare ourselves with others is through learning how to praise ourselves for our unique, intrinsic value.

A common concern about self-praise is that it may lead to arrogance, probably due to our Judeo-Christian tradition in which self-humiliation is often regarded as a necessary virtue to praise God, while self-praise is deemed to be a sign of pride, which is one of the seven deadly sins. It should be noted, however, that arrogance is a defensive posture caused by a tendency to assume a sense of superiority or inferiority by comparing oneself with others. Therefore, so long as we praise ourselves solely for who we are and for our innate Buddhahood, we will never become arrogant, though we may at times seem arrogant to arrogant people.

Indeed, the greatest way to praise ourselves is prayer that sincerely affirms our supreme potential. As Nichiren writes, "When you chant *myoho* and recite *renge*, you must summon up deep faith that Myoho-renge-kyo is your life itself" (WND, 3).

As we praise ourselves in this way, we will grow confident yet humble because we can recognize the same quality of Buddhahood in others as well. Through the practice of Nichiren Buddhism, appreciation for oneself leads to appreciation for others, which further strengthens self-esteem. The way we see ourselves is not only the way we live our lives but also the way we relate to others.

(from the November 9, 2001, *World Tribune*)

FOOD FOR THOUGHT:

✦ Some may feel that self-praise undermines self-discipline. Strictness, however, may come from either compassion or anger. What is the benefit of being strict with ourselves out of compassion rather than anger?

✦ Competition drives society. But why are some competitive people successful yet insecure? What is the weakness of a life built upon a sense of superiority?

KEY POINTS FOR CHAPTER 4

1) One of the greatest obstacles to the joy of loving is our desire for control. To master the art of loving is to overcome this selfish desire.

2) It is easy to mistake control and dependency for love. The truth of love, however, is found in our sincerity to act for the happiness and freedom of others.

3) To love truly, we must free ourselves from the fundamental darkness within—in other words, our denial of our own enlightenment. Authentic love begins with our innate sense of self-worth.

CHAPTER 4

What Love Is Not

"LOVE IS NOT LOVE" (Sonnet 116). As Shakespeare writes, what seems to be love may not be love at all. As much as the subject of love occupies many people's minds (and perhaps much of their time and money), their greatest concern appears to be confined to finding love or becoming lovable in the eyes of others, rather than the meaning of love or the capacity for loving.

The underlying assumption of this attitude may be that love is a feeling of pleasure and comfort stimulated only by an external object. The usual remedy for life without love, therefore, is to find someone new and better.

Erich Fromm, a noted psychologist and social philosopher, considers love an art that "requires knowledge and effort"; he defines love as "the active concern for the life and the growth of that which we love" (*The Art of Loving*, pp. 1, 25). If love is one's capacity to wish and act for the happiness and freedom of another person, a fundamental solution to the suffering of love must be sought not outward but in the development of the character and inner strength that make us capable of loving more genuinely and powerfully.

Mastering the Art of Loving

One of the greatest obstacles to the joy of loving is our desire for control. People sometimes mistake their wish to control others for loving concern. They may think of themselves as affectionate, yet their "love" may be a disguised desire to manipulate others for personal gain. In his writings, Nichiren Daishonin often uses a mythic Buddhist creature called the devil king of the sixth heaven as a metaphor for the deep-seated human desire to control others. Indeed, another name for this devil king (Jpn *takejizaiten*) literally means the "heavenly being who makes free use of others." Through his lively descriptions of this devil, Nichiren indicates the importance of becoming aware and vigilant of our desire to use others as a means to our selfish ends.

Since dependency is essential to control, the devil king uses various schemes to make people dependent on him. One of his main tools to encourage dependency is manipulation through feigned affection. Despite the general perception of the devil king as a fierce monster, he is adept at appearing affectionate. To lure people and keep them under his control, the devil king is said to make himself look like a Buddha or parent.

For example, Nichiren writes, "The devil king of the sixth heaven is endowed with the Buddha's thirty-two features and manifests the Buddha's body" (GZ, 114). He also quotes from a Buddhist commentary, which states, "So long as a person does not try to depart from the sufferings of birth and death and aspire to the Buddha vehicle, the devil will watch over him like a parent" (WND, 770). In fact, there is even a type of devil in the Buddhist tradition called "the devil of compassion" (GZ, 526).

Those who are eager to control others often appear affectionate with the aim of keeping others dependent materially or emotionally. In Ibsen's play *A Doll's House*, the seemingly affectionate yet controlling husband Torvald Helmer reminds his wife, Nora, of his "love" expressed in the form of financial support: "My pretty little pet is very sweet, but it runs away with an awful lot of money. It's incredible how expensive it is for a man to keep such a pet" (*Henrik Ibsen: Four Major Plays*, trans., James McFarlane and Jens Arup, p. 4).

The Truth of Love

It is easy to mistake control and dependency for love. The appearance of selfish love, like that of the devil king's, is deceptive, for its selfishness does not show as long as the recipient of such feigned affection remains submissive. As Nichiren points out, the devil king is affectionate "so long as a person does not try to depart from" his control (WND, 770). Some people may give anything to their "loved ones" only to keep them dependent.

Those obsessed with control, however, usually find it difficult to wish for the genuine happiness and independence of others. Instead, they hope to see others deprived in one way or another in order to maintain their sense of superiority and control. As Nichiren writes, "The nature of this devil king is to rejoice at those who create the karma of the three evil paths and to grieve at those who form the karma of the three good paths" (WND, 42).

The test of our love, in this sense, lies in our sincerity to encourage and work for the self-reliance and freedom of our loved ones. Those who thrive on domination may easily show pity for others in suffering, while inwardly delighting at the sight. The misery of others affords those in control yet another opportunity to show their superiority and thereby remind those suffering of their need for dependency.

At the core of a relationship built on domination and submission lies a profound sense of insecurity and powerlessness on both sides. Those who like to dominate cannot accept their existence on their own, so they must derive a sense of power by subjugating others. Similarly, those who easily submit to an external authority cannot see their self-worth, so they feel compelled to become part of someone "better" and "stronger" by abandoning their identity and integrity.

To such submissive people, control means protection against their own insecurity. Those submissive to an external authority do not see their lives as worthwhile, nor can they endure the emptiness of having no one for whom to live. Instead, they must seek an external object with which to merge their identity to avoid facing the weakness and emptiness of their lives.

This symbiotic relationship between the dominant and the submissive is disturbed when the submissive party uncovers his or her self-worth and develops the inner strength to become independent. Then the dominant party's insecurity will surface as frustration and anger.

Nichiren's following descriptions illustrate the devil king's intense fear and anxiety in this regard: "When we thus draw near to achieving Buddhahood...the devil king of the sixth heaven, lord of the threefold world, reasons: 'If these persons should become Buddhas, I will suffer loss on two counts. First of all, if they free themselves from the threefold world, they will escape my control. Second, if they become Buddhas, their parents and siblings will also depart from the saha world. How can I stop this from happening?'" (WND, 1094). "When an ordinary person of the latter age is ready to attain Buddhahood...this devil is greatly surprised. He says to himself, 'This is most vexing. If I allow this person to remain in my domain, he not only will free himself from the sufferings of birth and death, but will lead others to enlightenment as well. Moreover, he will take over my realm and change it into a pure land. What shall I do?'" (WND, 894).

To Love Truly

The devil king does not want anyone to attain enlightenment and become free since that would be a painful reminder of his own powerlessness and dependency. The paradox of this devil king, who "dwells at the summit of the world of desire and rules over the threefold world" (WND, 508), is that he is controlled by his own desire to control. The devil king is a ruler who cannot rule himself. The more control he has, the more of it he needs. He is perpetually driven by his inner weakness and insecurity, never feeling satisfied. He is a prisoner of the prison he himself creates. Although he is said to make "free use of others," he is never free in the innermost reality of his life. The devil king, therefore, is incapable of loving.

The devil king is said to dwell in the sixth and highest heaven of the world of desire, but his "love" results only in profound unfulfillment and suffering beneath its heavenly pleasure. As William Blake knew, such selfish "Love seeketh only Self to please, / To bind another to Its delight: / Joys in anothers loss of ease, / And builds a Hell in Heavens despite" ("The Clod & the Pebble," *The Complete Poetry and Prose of William Blake*, David V. Erdman, ed., p. 19).

To love truly, we must be free. To be free, then, we must discover our innate self-worth. In Shakespeare's sonnet quoted earlier, he also wrote, "Let me not to the marriage of true minds / Admit impediments." One of the greatest impediments to our ability to love is delusion about the truth of our inner life—Buddhahood. Such delusion leads to powerlessness and dependency. The mythic devil king is symbolic of this delusion. As Nichiren writes, "The fundamental darkness manifests itself as the devil king of the sixth heaven" (WND, 1113). To shed light on this fundamental darkness through strengthening our confidence in Buddhahood, then, is an essential practice for the art of loving.

(from the December 7, 2001, *World Tribune*)

FOOD FOR THOUGHT:

+ Why do you think some people are more concerned about becoming lovable or finding love rather than developing the capacity to love more profoundly and authentically?

+ In what ways has your Nichiren Buddhist practice enabled you to love more profoundly and authentically?

+ Nichiren Daishonin saw the workings of the devil king of the sixth heaven in his own life (see WND, 310). What did you learn about yourself from the story of the devil king? How do you relate to his selfishness and insecurity?

KEY POINTS FOR CHAPTER 5

1) Faith must be freely chosen. If faith is coerced, it becomes hypocritical. Nichiren Buddhism teaches that to compromise one's freedom of conscience is to abandon one's personal integrity.

2) Honest, open dialogue is a concrete expression of faith and freedom. Through speaking what we believe as truth and listening to the viewpoints of others, we can develop mutual respect among different faiths based on understanding.

3) To enjoy the freedom of religion, we must overcome our inner powerlessness and awaken to our true conscience. For without inner strength, we become vulnerable to external powers and their manipulation of our conscience.

CHAPTER 5

Faith and Freedom

Congress shall make no law respecting an establishment of religion, or prohibiting the free exercise thereof.
—THE FIRST AMENDMENT, UNITED STATES CONSTITUTION

SGI shall, based on the Buddhist spirit of tolerance, respect other religions, engage in dialogue and work together with them toward the resolution of fundamental issues concerning humanity.
—ARTICLE 7, THE SGI CHARTER

TO EXERCISE FREEDOM of religion, as guaranteed by the First Amendment, is to choose and practice religion freely according to one's conscience. We exercise this freedom when we make a conscious decision to take faith, uninhibited by any external power. I exercised my freedom of religion when I was twenty-one, although my family had joined the Soka Gakkai almost two decades earlier.

When I was a senior in college, one of my best friends developed cancer and was given a year to live. I was desperate, not knowing what I could do for him.

I spoke with an SGI leader whom I respected. He said,

"Let's introduce your friend to Nichiren Buddhism!" So I did.

After I visited him at the hospital for more than forty days in a row, my friend decided to join the SGI, not because my explanation of Buddhism had made any sense to him, but probably because he thought he had nothing to lose at that point. To make our long story short, he eventually overcame his illness. Today, almost twenty years later, he still practices Buddhism despite his busy work schedule. He is healthy and happily married with two children.

The process of encouraging my friend to take faith was the process of my own awakening. I witnessed the power of prayer as he became healthier. I also witnessed the sincerity of many SGI members who supported my friend as if he were their own son. At that time, I decided to practice Nichiren Buddhism for my own sake. That was the moment I exercised my freedom of religion. It is ironic that when I thought I was helping my friend, he was actually helping me to make one of the most important decisions of my life. I freely chose to practice this faith through my own experience and understanding, however limited at that time.

Faith Needs Freedom

Faith must be freely chosen. If faith is coerced, whatever one professes cannot be called "faith" anymore. In his Latin treatise *A Letter Concerning Toleration*, John Locke writes: "All the life and power of true religion consist in the inward and full persuasion of the mind; and faith is not faith without believing" (Patrick Romanell, ed., William Popple, trans., p. 18). Locke went so far as to assert that the coercion of faith is not only "hypocrisy" but also "contempt" of religion itself (ibid., 18). True religious faith cannot exist without freedom of religion, whose quintessence lies in freedom of conscience.

Nichiren Daishonin understood the importance of individual conscience and held that the realm of faith is above and beyond the reach of any secular power. As he proclaimed to Hei no Saemon, a powerful military official of the Kamakura shogunate government, "Even if it seems that, because I was born in the ruler's domain, I follow him in my actions, I will never follow him in my heart" (WND, 579). Nichiren knew that to compromise one's freedom of conscience is to abandon one's personal integrity and lead a life of hypocrisy. So he encouraged his own disciples: "My disciples, form your ranks and follow me.... If you quail before the threats of the ruler of this little island country [and abandon your faith], how will you face the even more terrible anger of Yama, the lord of hell? If, while calling yourselves the Buddha's messengers, you give way to fear, you will be the most despicable of persons!" (WND, 765).

James Madison, the prime author of the First Amendment, also understood freedom of conscience as the foundation of faith. In his "Memorial and Remonstrance Against Religious Assessments," Madison argued against a proposed tax to support Christian ministers of all denomina-

tions. He writes: "Religion or the duty which we owe to
our Creator and the manner of discharging it, can be
directed only by reason and conviction, not by force or violence. The Religion then of every man must be left to the
conviction and conscience of every man; and it is the right
of every man to exercise it as these may dictate. This right is
in its nature an unalienable right. It is unalienable, because
the opinions of men, depending only on the evidence con-
templated by their own minds cannot follow the dictates of
other men" (*James Madison: Writings*, p. 30). Freedom of religion exists so that it may protect and encourage freedom of
conscience. For without freedom of conscience, there can
be no faith.

The outer shell of religion may flourish without freedom
of religion, but the substance of religion cannot survive
without it. Madison explains that the absence of religious
freedom and the influence of external powers lead to "pride
and indolence in the Clergy, ignorance and servility in the
laity, in both, superstition, bigotry and persecution" (ibid.,
32).

Freedom Needs Faith

For faith to thrive, one's conscience must be free. Freedom
of conscience, in turn, depends upon one's inner strength
of character. Those who lack spiritual strength may be easily swayed by the threat and fear of an external power and
confused by the manipulations of others. As a means of

spiritual empowerment, people have often depended on their faith. As much as faith needs freedom, freedom needs faith, because freedom presupposes strength of spirit, which seeks as its source the engine of faith.

Alexis de Tocqueville, one of the most astute observers of American democracy, saw another reason why freedom needs faith: "Religion, which, among Americans, never mixes directly in the government of society, should therefore be considered as the first of their political institutions; for if it does not give them the taste for freedom, it singularly facilitates their use of it" (*Democracy in America*, Harvey C. Mansfield and Delba Winthrop, trans., p. 280). What is the use of freedom, Tocqueville argues, if we lack its prime outlet of expression? We can enjoy the fruit of liberty with a great sense of immediacy when we experience freedom in our choice and practice of faith. Because we cherish faith, we value and fight for the liberty upon which faith depends. As much as our democracy needs freedom, our freedom needs faith. In this sense, there is a profound significance in Tocqueville's statement that religion is "the first" of America's "political institutions." Religion, in Tocqueville's opinion, is the foundation of America's freedom and thus its democracy.

An Expression of Faith and Freedom

Our honest, open dialogue with others is a concrete expression of our faith and freedom; it is one of the most important forms of the free exercise of religion guaranteed by the First Amendment for all Americans. Through speaking what we believe as truth and listening to the viewpoints of others, we can develop mutual respect among different faiths based on understanding instead of inciting hatred based on ignorance.

The exercise of religious freedom, however, should not be without bounds. One cannot inflict violence on others, claiming that doing so is one's free exercise of religion. No one can refuse to pay taxes in America, claiming that paying taxes goes against one's religious beliefs. These are external bounds of religious freedom set by the laws of society.

In addition, there are some internal forms of the abuse of religious freedom that, though they may not go against the laws of society, contradict the purpose and intent of religious freedom. If a person, engaged in a dialogue about faith, tries to manipulate another's conscience and obstruct his or her exercise of reason through fear or falsehood, that person is contradicting the purpose of dialogue by causing confusion instead of understanding.

In this sense, one important purpose of our dialogue on faith is to encourage the free exercise of conscience through appealing to others' reason and integrity. To respect others and their religions is to respect their power and responsibility to make up their own minds.

Beyond Negative Freedom and Passive Tolerance

Although we have religious liberty, there are some limits to how our Founding Fathers enabled us to truly enjoy "the free exercise thereof." An influential British philosopher of the last century, Isaiah Berlin explained that there are two kinds of freedom: "negative freedom" and "positive freedom" ("Two Concepts of Liberty" from *Four Essays on Liberty*, pp. 118–72). What he describes as negative freedom is freedom from external constraints, which are usually political in nature. Berlin calls such freedom "negative" not necessarily because it is lower in value, but because it is essentially a release from external forces and conditions. Positive freedom, on the other hand, is freedom to do something in accord with one's conscience. Berlin explains that positive freedom is the freedom of a "doer—deciding, not being decided for, self-directed and not acted upon by external nature or by other men" (ibid., 131).

In America, we enjoy the precious, hard-won negative freedom from government powers in matters of religion, thanks to Madison and other fighters of religious liberty. To enjoy the positive freedom of religion, however, each of us must work to overcome our inner powerlessness and awaken to our true conscience. Without inner strength, we are vulnerable to external powers and their manipulation of our conscience. We would let others decide matters of faith for us instead of deciding on our own.

Another hurdle to overcome for the true enjoyment of

religious freedom is passive tolerance. Passive tolerance is indifference to others' happiness; it is the lack of compassion that says: "Do whatever you please. It's your own concern. But don't meddle in my business." Genuine tolerance is the opposite of indifference; it is an active concern and respect for the happiness of others.

To go beyond negative freedom and passive tolerance, people need to strengthen themselves and develop compassion for others. In this sense, to further deepen the idea and practice of religious liberty in America, we practice Nichiren Buddhism. Our efforts to engage in dialogue with others are not only an expression of freedom afforded by the Founding Fathers but also a historic enterprise to give substance to this American ideal.

(from the February 15, 2002, *World Tribune*)

FOOD FOR THOUGHT:

✦ While utmost courtesy and decency must be observed in dialogue, speaking out the truth of Nichiren Buddhism is the essence of the Soka Spirit. What understanding and attitude will enable us to refute the misleading beliefs of Nichiren Shoshu with respect?

✦ It is difficult to separate persons from their ideas since people often feel offended when their beliefs are criticized. Not to offend others, therefore, some people avoid dialogue on faith altogether. How can we overcome this obstacle in our path of dialogue without eliminating the path itself?

✦ It's easy to be tolerant if you don't believe. It's often the case that the stronger your religious conviction, the more intolerant you become. What aspects of Nichiren Buddhism make it possible that the more you believe, the more genuinely tolerant you become?

Key Points for Chapter 6

1) Authoritarian religion emphasizes the power of external authority and uses the fear of death to manipulate people. The current Nichiren Shoshu priesthood promotes this tradition of "funeral Buddhism."

2) Nichiren Daishonin emphasizes practitioners' own faith in triumphing over death. Nowhere in his writings does he say that priests' rituals and prayers are essential for the enlightenment of practitioners, whether living or dead. Instead he emphasizes his followers' sincere practice in the here and now for their happiness and the peace of the deceased.

CHAPTER 6

The Business of Death

ONE OF THE EASIEST WAYS to manipulate people is through fear. Since the fear of death is the greatest fear for most people, many religionists have long exploited death as a means to manipulate believers for their selfish gain.

For example, the sale of indulgences by "pardoners" grew considerably from the later Middle Ages and became an immediate cause for the Protestant Reformation. In his "Disputation on the Power and Efficacy of Indulgences," commonly known as "The Ninety-five Theses," posted on a church door in Wittenberg in 1517, Martin Luther writes, "There is no divine authority for preaching that the soul flies out of purgatory immediately the money clinks in the bottom of the chest" (*Martin Luther: Selections from His Writings*, John Dillenberger, ed., p. 493).

Neither was the history of Buddhism immune to the clerical exploitation of people's fear of death. The late fifteenth century saw the economic growth of farmers in Japan. Now that many farmers did not have to worry so much about starvation, they began thinking of their afterlife and adopted funeral rites, which had been previously reserved for aristocrats and samurai warriors. Buddhist priests were quick to seize this opportunity; they began to systematize funeral rites and invented dogmas to stress the importance of having priests conduct services for the deceased.

Priests Created "Funeral Buddhism"

In order to stress their role as officiators of funeral rites, some priests of Nichiren Buddhism went so far as to forge documents and attribute them to their founder. One such document, titled "On the Blessings of Funeral Rites" (Jpn *Eko kudoku sho*), vividly describes the gruesome agonies of the dead and explains that their surviving families must ask priests to perform funeral rites in order to relieve their pains. This document puts the following words in the mouth of Nichiren Daishonin: "According to the Nirvana Sutra, King Yama [of hell], upon some considerations, drives forty-nine nails into the dead. Nevertheless, if they have pious children in this world and send someone for a priest to pray for their repose, this news will be brought to the palace of King Yama, and immediately fifteen nails will be removed from their feet" (*Showa Teihon Nichiren Shonin Imon*, p. 53; this document is also included in *Showa Shintei Nichiren Daishonin Gosho* published by Nichiren Shoshu). There is no such description in the Nirvana Sutra as the author of this forged document claims.

According to this writing, each of the forty-nine nails driven into the dead is as long as one foot. When a priest transcribes a sutra passage on a memorial tablet upon his arrival, six nails will be removed from the stomach. When a priest conducts consecration—called "eye-opening"—on the tablet, eighteen nails will be removed from the chest. When he delivers a sermon for the dead, two nails will be removed from the ears. When a priest prays to the tablet, two more will be removed from the eyes. And when the surviving family members chant Nam-myoho-renge-kyo to this consecrated memorial tablet, the last six nails will be removed from the tongue.

This forgery also warns believers: "Although you have been bequeathed with the belongings of your father and mother, if you neglect to perform the funeral rites for their repose, thinking that the dead can do nothing, then the dead will become evil spirits and haunt their descendants generation after generation" (ibid., 56). The priestly author of the document cleverly plays upon believers' ignorance of Buddhism, inciting their guilt for failing to perform filial duties and their fear of the afterlife. Moreover, the author claims that if believers do not pay priests to perform those elaborate funeral rites, they will be tormented by the dead even in this world. Without priests' help, he warns, believers' worldly pleasure and comfort will be eclipsed by the shadow of underworld.

The current Nichiren Shoshu priesthood continues this tradition of "funeral Buddhism." On October 21, 1991, about one month before excommunicating the Soka Gakkai, then Nichiren Shoshu General Administrator Nichijun

Fujimoto sent "Notification" to Soka Gakkai President
Einosuke Akiya. In it, Mr. Fujimoto writes: "Recently the
Soka Gakkai has been conducting funerals for its member-
ship without priests.... This is a slanderous act to destroy
the Daishonin's Buddhism.... Nichiren Shoshu, therefore,
absolutely cannot condone it." Mr. Fujimoto went on to
declare in his notification that those who conduct funerals
without priests—as well as the deceased—"will surely fall
into hell."

In Nichiren Buddhism, however, the funeral rites con-
ducted by priests were never intended as essential to the
enlightenment of the deceased. Instead, Nichiren emphasizes practitioners' own faith to triumph in death. For
example, he writes: "Nam-myoho-renge-kyo will be your
staff to take you safely over the mountain of death....
Devote yourself single-mindedly to faith with the aim of
reaching Eagle Peak" (WND, 451–52).

Nowhere in his writings does Nichiren mention that
priests' rituals and prayers are essential for the enlightenment of practitioners, whether living or dead. Nichiren
emphasizes his followers' sincere practice in the here and
now—for their own happiness as well as for the peace of
the deceased. He consistently drives home the importance
of faith: "What is most important is that, by chanting Nam-
myoho-renge-kyo alone, you can attain Buddhahood. It
will no doubt depend on the strength of your faith. To have
faith is the basis of Buddhism" (WND, 832).

A False Sense of Security

Many philosophers in the past tried to explain away the fear of death. For example, Epicurus, an ancient Greek philosopher, taught that the fear of death is irrational. As he argued: "So death, the most frightening of bad things, is nothing to us; since when we exist, death is not yet present, and when death is present, then we do not exist" (*The Epicurus Reader: Selected Writings and Testimonia*, Brad Inwood and L. P. Gerson, trans. and ed., p. 29). Epicurus, however, admitted that the majority of people are gripped by the fear of death: "One can attain security against other things, but when it comes to death all men live in a city without walls" (ibid., 37).

No matter how we may try to rationalize death, the fear of death seems to creep up from the depths of our existences. Some leave matters of death to the so-called professionals, such as priests or spiritualists, and go on living in complete oblivion to their approaching deaths. Others try to numb their fear of death by seeking a false sense of security in the reward of an afterlife or release from present sufferings rather than face death and search for life's meaning therein.

Authoritarian religion thrives on people's inability to deal with death; it uses the idea of an afterlife as an escape from the reality of death rather than as encouragement to confront and triumph over the inevitable end of our present existence. Teaching that there is an afterlife, however, does not make a religion authoritarian. For example, the Buddhist concept of life's eternity can be used either as an escape from the reality of death or as a tool to understand death and create value in life. Depending on our emphasis—whether on powers outside people or powers within people, we may make an authoritarian dogma even out of a humanistic religion.

Authoritarian religion emphasizes the power of external authority and uses the fear of death to manipulate people, as we see in the sale of indulgences or the funeral rites of some Japanese Buddhist sects. Nichiren was especially strict toward clergy who promoted esoteric rituals and undermined lay believers' self-reliant faith: "The priests of today observe the two hundred and fifty precepts in name only and, in fact, use their so-called observance of the precepts as a means to dupe others. They have not a trace of transcendental power—a huge stone could sooner ascend to heaven than they could exercise such powers. Their wisdom is in a class with that of oxen, no different from that of sheep. Though they might gather together by the thousands or ten thousands, they could never relieve one iota of the sufferings of departed parents" (WND, 819).

To Face the Fear of Death

To understand the meaning of death and overcome our fear of it, we need the strength to face our final reality. Regarding our escapist attitude toward death, Martin Heidegger, a German existentialist philosopher, writes: "One *knows* about the certainty of death, and yet 'is' not authentically certain of one's own.... One says, 'Death certainly comes, but not right away.' With this 'but...,' the 'they' denies that death is certain.... Death is deferred to 'sometime later.'... Thus the 'they' covers up what is peculiar in death's certainty—*that it is possible at any moment*" (*Being and Time*, John Macquarrie and Edward Robinson, trans., p. 302). Heidegger, in this regard, describes our existence as "Being-towards-death"; that is, "dying factically and indeed constantly, as long as it has not yet come to its demise" (ibid., 303).

Humanistic religion stresses our inner strength and encourages us to face our reality as "Being-towards-death." Erich Fromm, a noted psychoanalyst of the last century, explains: "Humanistic religion...is centered around man and his strength.... Man's aim in humanistic religion is to achieve the greatest strength, not the greatest powerlessness; virtue is self-realization, not obedience" (*Psychoanalysis and Religion*, p. 37). Nichiren Buddhism is intended to do what Fromm envisioned in humanistic religion—to help people awaken to their inner strength and thus overcome any obstacle, including death.

In this regard, Nichiren states in *The Record of the Orally Transmitted Teachings*: "To look on birth and death with repulsion and try to escape from them is termed delusion.... Seeing and understanding the originally inherent nature of birth and death is termed awakening.... Now when Nichiren and his followers chant Nam-myoho-renge-kyo, they realize the originally inherent nature of birth and death, and the originally inherent nature of ebb and flow" (p. 127).

To understand death as an innate working of life is a path not only toward triumph over death but also toward enlightened living. Here, Nichiren teaches that understanding both life and death as the two inherent aspects of our existence through chanting Nam-myoho-renge-kyo is essential to our complete happiness.

Instead of deluding ourselves into a fiction of death as reserved only for someone else or to occur at some distant, imagined future, Nichiren encourages us to face our present reality as "Being-towards-death" by cultivating "the profound insight that now is the last moment of one's life" (WND, 216). The meaning of death, according to Nichiren, lies in our current efforts to live to the fullest extent. Our prayer to the Gohonzon, therefore, should be our affirmation of life in the face of death. As Nichiren writes, "Be resolved to summon forth the great power of faith, and chant Nam-myoho-renge-kyo with the prayer that your faith will be steadfast and correct at the moment of death" (WND, 218). Through such powerful prayer and dedication, Nichiren teaches, we can discover a true sense of security deeply grounded in the reality of life and death.

As long as we feel powerless in the face of the essential reality that death is possible at any moment, we will find a way to deny death and thereby deny the reality of life. Life lived without an awareness of death is life lived in unreality. It may be easy to blame corrupt priests for exploiting people's fear of death, but the real blame lies in people's powerlessness to face the reality of death. As long as we live in denial of death, there will always be scandalous religionists who make their business out of death. To live a life rooted in reality, however, each of us must learn to take care of the business of death ourselves. For the business of death is the most important business of life.

(from the March 22, 2002, *World Tribune*)

FOOD FOR THOUGHT:

✦ Nichiren writes, "One must learn about death and then learn about other matters" (GZ, 1404). Unless we are extremely old or suffering from terminal disease, we rarely think of our death as an inevitable, approaching reality. As foolish as it is to be paralyzed by the fear of death, it is equally unfortunate to live in complete denial of death. What do you think we need to do to face death as our most intimate reality and transform it into a springboard for more fulfilled living?

✦ It is easier to accept death in resignation than to fight for life with the awareness of death's certainty. How can we encourage ourselves and others—especially when faced with serious illnesses—to accept death with hope and still continue living with courage? What does SGI President Ikeda mean when he says, "Sustained faith and practice enable us to know a deep and abiding joy in death as well as in life" (*My Dear Friends in America*, p. 334)?

KEY POINTS FOR CHAPTER 7

1) Seeking salvation outside or pilgrimage to a sacred site has no place in Nichiren Buddhism. What is most important is confidence in our inherent Buddhahood.

2) We doubt our Buddha nature because of our ignorance and habitual self-disparagement. Our honest self-reflection and persistent faith will help us break through such doubt and discover the gem of Buddhahood within.

3) Our Buddhist practice in the here and now enables us to reveal our innate Buddhahood. There is no distance between our lives and the truth of Nichiren Buddhism.

CHAPTER 7

The "Pilgrim's Progress"— From Without to Within

Midway in the journey of our life I found myself in a dark wood, for the straight way was lost.

—DANTE

MOST OF US enjoy visiting exotic places. Despite long lines at airports and travel warnings issued by the State Department, we still yearn to stand on the Incan ruins at Machu Picchu or daydream of lounging on a Tahitian beach. Of course, when we leave town, we want to relax and have fun. Leisure, however, does not seem to be the only element behind our passion for travel.

When we leave behind our mundane responsibilities and wake up one morning thousands of miles away from home, we sometimes get in touch with a part of us that has been long forgotten through many years of daily routine. So when we come home, we somehow feel refreshed and more wholesome, despite jetlag and swollen feet.

A good trip, in this way, works like a good work of art. Like reading *Don Quixote* or listening to *The Ode to Joy*, a truly rewarding trip is one that helps us discover more of ourselves. On the contrary, a mediocre trip, although it may be full of frivolous fun, lacks this joy of self-discovery and self-renewal. This may be due more to the difference in attitude between a traveler seeking new knowledge and a tourist waiting to be entertained, rather than to the difference in distance or destination.

We Are Strangers to Ourselves

Our desire to travel to a far-off land is deeply related to our yearning to reunite with something important or even sacred from which we feel alienated. Our passion for travel, in this sense, is almost religious. This may be one of the chief reasons for the popular union of travel and faith—that is, pilgrimage.

In most major religions of the world, believers throughout the centuries have made a journey to their sacred places as an act of devotion: for example, Christians and Jews to Jerusalem; Muslims to Mecca; Hindus to Benares; Buddhists to Bodh Gaya and so forth. Furthermore, countless local shrines and temples the world over are visited by their devotees every year. People's attachment to these holy sites is so strong and, at times, misguided that much blood has been spilt in drawing and redrawing their boundaries to this day.

The etymologies of the words *religion* and *pilgrimage* suggest our essential motive for undertaking a journey of faith, as language often shapes and is shaped by the people who use it. The word *religion* is related to the Latin verb *religare*, that is, "to tie back" or "to unite," and the word *pilgrimage* to the Latin verb *peregrinari*, that is, "to travel abroad" or "to be a stranger." The linguistic origins of those words imply that we somehow feel like a stranger in the world we live in. So we leave our homes and travel abroad in search of something from which we have been estranged.

Our fundamental religious impulse, in other words, derives from our sense of aloneness and alienation. One historian writes, "The desire to be a pilgrim is deeply rooted in human nature" (Steven Runciman, *A History of the Crusades*, vol. 1, p. 38). Thus, we see ourselves as strangers who wander through foreign lands, seeking to unite with something precious we have lost.

In many ways, people try hard to overcome this sense of separation—the cause of which, however, they are unable to pinpoint. Some seek solace in their supposed saviors in heaven while others in the objects of their desires here on earth. The Lotus Sutra, however, identifies that from which we are alienated as our innate Buddhahood. It teaches that our true longing is neither for a god living above us nor for a perfect lover ever eluding our grasp.

After many years or even lifetimes of deluded self-disparagement (in other words, the slander of the Law), we have become strangers to ourselves, specifically, to our true self, that is, the universal Buddha nature within us. A fundamental way to overcome our sense of separation, therefore, is to see ourselves for what we truly are and tap into the most essential part of our lives. The Lotus Sutra metaphorically illustrates this point through the parable of the gem in the robe.

Transforming Pilgrimage and Worship

In the "Prophecy of Enlightenment for Five Hundred Disciples" chapter of the sutra, the Buddha's disciples—reflecting upon their previous ignorance of "comprehensive wisdom"—tell the following parable: "World-Honored One, it was like the case of a man who went to the house of a close friend and, having become drunk on wine, lay down to sleep. At that time the friend had to go out on official business. He took a priceless jewel, sewed it in the lining of the man's robe, and left it with him when he went out. The man was asleep drunk and knew nothing about it. When he got up, he set out on a journey to other countries. In order to provide himself with food and clothing he had to search with all his energy and diligence, encountering very great hardship and making do with what little he could come by. Later, the close friend happened to meet him by chance. The friend said, 'How absurd, old fellow! Why should you have to do all this for the sake of food and clothing? In the past I wanted to make certain you would be able to live in ease and satisfy the five desires, and so on such-and-such a day and month and year I took a priceless jewel and sewed it in the lining of your robe. It must still be there now. But you did not know about it, and fretted and wore yourself out trying to provide a living for yourself. What nonsense! Now you must take the jewel and exchange it for goods. Then you can have whatever you wish at all times and never experience poverty or want'" (LS, 150–51).

In this parable, the good friend represents the Buddha, and the priceless jewel sewed in the lining of the poor man's robe our innate Buddha nature hidden in the depths of our lives. The poor man is symbolic of the "pilgrim" in all of us, who wanders through life in search of true happiness. His tragedy is that, despite the "energy and diligence" he exerts, he meets nothing but "very great hardship" without ever feeling satisfied. His problem is his ignorance; he is looking for the source of fulfillment in the wrong place— outside himself.

Just like this poor man, we often seek in vain our self-worth in status, material possessions or the approval of others—whether they are parents or partners or supposed saviors or saints. The last place we look is our own lives, for we judge ourselves by the tattered clothes of temporary setbacks in life and delude ourselves into believing that there is no intrinsic value to our lives.

Regarding this parable, Nichiren Daishonin explains that the wine that the poor man drinks is symbolic of his ignorance of his innate Buddhahood, and his drunken state is symbolic of being "lacking in faith" in his innate Buddhahood (see OTT, 78–79). He also comments, "Now, when

Nichiren and his followers chant Nam-myoho-renge-kyo, they are in effect sobering up from the wine of ignorance" (ibid.).

Here Nichiren declares that through devoting ourselves to the chanting of Nam-myoho-renge-kyo with confidence in our innate Buddhahood, we begin to experience the power of the priceless jewel inside us and live our lives as Buddhas—as persons of genuine strength and courage who are capable of building their own happiness while encouraging others to do the same. As Nichiren suggests, the Lotus Sutra's "comprehensive wisdom" that enables us to see the priceless jewel of Buddhahood inside can be found in and cultivated through confidence in our Buddha nature and the practice of chanting Nam-myoho-renge-kyo.

Through the parable of the gem in the robe, the Lotus Sutra underscores the futility of searching for the source of fulfillment outside ourselves. It may be significant to note that the Lotus Sutra is an outgrowth of the Mahayana Buddhist movement, which is said to have evolved from the popular practice of visiting a Buddhist memorial mound or tower called stupa and worshiping the Buddha's relics supposedly enshrined inside. The sutra, however, transcends the limitations of its historical origin.

Through describing the appearance of the magnificent treasure tower beyond any earthly measure as a metaphor of our innate Buddha nature, the Lotus Sutra directs our gaze from a stupa outside to the treasure tower inside. Also, through stories such as the gem in the robe, the sutra stresses the importance of self-awakening instead of salvation from outside. The Lotus Sutra, therefore, marks a Copernican transformation of the idea of pilgrimage and worship from one that is directed *outside* oneself to one that is directed *within*.

In fact, the Lotus Sutra refutes people's attachment to sacred sites and particular places of worship. In the sutra, its votaries foretell their future: "Again and again we will be banished / to a place far removed from towers and temples" (LS, 195). Despite exile and persecution, those votaries of the sutra pledge to spread its teaching far and wide. Their connection with Buddhism is not tied to any particular place nor does their relationship with the Buddha depend on any sentimentality attached to his physical presence or his relics.

Instead, what links those votaries with their teacher and his teaching is their resolve to practice and spread Buddhism with the same spirit. As they proclaim in verse:

> *If in the settlements and towns*
> *There are those who seek the Law,*
> *We will go to wherever they are*
> *And preach the Law entrusted to us by the Buddha.*
> *We will be envoys of the World-Honored One,*
> *Facing the assembly without fear....*
> *We proclaim this vow.*
> *The Buddha must know what is in our hearts.* (LS, 195)

The Lotus Sutra makes it clear that Buddhism lives on not in "towers and temples" but in its practitioners' vow to spread the Buddhist wisdom of self-discovery and self-renewal for the ordinary people living in "settlements and towns."

During the first century of the Common Era, in which the Lotus Sutra is said to have been compiled, those "towers and temples" in India generally indicated stupas and structures surrounding them. As people revered and worshiped the Buddha's relics supposedly enshrined inside, those Buddhist memorials came to be regarded as sacred sites and attracted many pilgrims, thus becoming an important source of income for clergy. The sutra predicts that its practitioners will be banished repeatedly from those supposedly sacred sites.

Through this episode of banishment, the compilers of the Lotus Sutra, as the reformers of Buddhism, probably wished to leave behind their own experiences in promoting the revival of the Buddha's true teaching while facing the opposition of clergy. The sutra, in this sense, seems to be asking us: Does Buddhism exist in sacred sites or in physical objects such as the Buddha's relics? Or does it come alive in the hearts and actions of practitioners dedicated to the happiness of people? The sutra's message, after two millennia, still rings with truth and urgency today.

An Inward Search for Buddhahood

What stands in our way as we search for the priceless gem of Buddhahood within is our doubt and fear. We doubt our Buddhahood because we are accustomed to disparaging ourselves. By the culture of competition and consumption, we are trained to think less of ourselves if we do not possess more than others—usually money, status and appearance. We fear and flee from our Buddhahood because it is easier to remain a victim of fate and circumstances, always blaming everything but ourselves rather than become makers of fate and circumstances who must self-reflect and bear the challenge of revealing our utmost potential.

Buddhas do not live *beyond* such delusions. Rather, Buddhas rise *above* their deep-seated doubt and fear of Buddhahood through courageous self-reflection and persistent faith in the essential self. Attaining Buddhahood, in this sense, is the process of overcoming doubt and fear through true self-knowledge. In the course of our Buddhist practice, therefore, we must clearly perceive and guard against whatever distracts us from this inward journey to find the priceless gem of Buddhahood.

In *The Pilgrim's Progress*, which remains one of the most influential Christian writings, John Bunyan uses dream allegory to describe the pilgrimage of an ordinary man called "Christian" from the City of Destruction to the Celestial City. Christian's spiritual pilgrimage "from this world to that which is to come"—as the book's subtitle reads—may be understood as a Protestant response to the medieval institution of pilgrimage, which was promoted by the Catholic Church and eventually degenerated through the abuse of relics and indulgences. In fact, pilgrimages were imposed by the Inquisition as penances for crimes and became part of civil and criminal law penalties (see Alan Kendall, *Medieval Pilgrims*, pp. 19, 109). Bunyan probably wished to correct such coercion and corruption of pilgrimage by stressing pilgrimage as the spiritual progress of a believer, not as earthly travel to receive remissions for sins or to worship relics. As an eighth-century Irish poem reads: "To go [to] Rome means great labour and little profit; the king you seek can only be found there if you bring him within yourself" (ibid., 12).

With a sense of endearment and nostalgia, we sometimes call those English families who founded the colony of Plymouth in 1620 "Pilgrim Fathers." The original settlers felt like pilgrims and strangers in the New World, and likewise many Americans still feel the same way—perhaps not in the external environment, but in their inner landscape of aloneness and alienation. The Lotus Sutra and Nichiren Buddhism, in this regard, may act as a guide to bring a sense of direction to America's spiritual wandering.

A genuine Buddhist pilgrimage—if such a word should exist in our vocabulary—is neither from our homes to a distant sacred place nor "from this world to that which is to come." With our consistent Buddhist faith and practice, we progress through doubt and fear toward the inner source of true happiness in the here and now and daily reach our destination of self-realization. Ours is a new kind of pilgrimage, one that reorients life's wandering without into life's discovery within.

(from the May 24, 2002, *World Tribune*)

FOOD FOR THOUGHT:

+ If attaining enlightenment is the ongoing process of overcoming our doubt and fear of Buddhahood, then recognizing these obstacles for what they are is to go more than halfway toward our mastery. In what ways do you experience doubt and fear of Buddhahood? And how do you challenge them?

+ In the parable of the gem in the robe, the poor man fortunately reunites with his good friend after many years of wandering. But what if he happens on someone who poses as his good friend yet further misguides his search of happiness away from his own Buddhahood? How can we tell an impostor from a genuine good friend in faith?

KEY POINTS FOR CHAPTER 8

1) Nichiren Daishonin stressed the importance of self-knowledge and inscribed the Gohonzon as a mirror to reflect our true self, our innate Buddhahood.

2) Genuine Nichiren Buddhists must not simply be admirers of the Gohonzon who see it with awe yet fail to see themselves in it. The true value of this wonderful mirror manifests through each practitioner's confidence in his or her innate Buddhahood.

CHAPTER 8

The Invisible Reflection

ØREN KIERKEGAARD, a Danish religious philosopher, knew the importance of seeing oneself in order to build a secure foundation for authentic happiness. So he suggested three requirements for his fellow Christians to see themselves in the "mirror" of "God's Word" (*For Self-Examination and Judge for Yourself!*, Howard V. Hong and Edna H. Hong, trans., p. 25).

Kierkegaard's insight into how to gain self-knowledge may be valuable not only for Christians but also for the practitioners of Nichiren Buddhism, since Nichiren Daishonin also stressed the importance of self-knowledge and inscribed the Gohonzon—the object of devotion in Nichiren Buddhism—as a mirror to reflect our true self, our innate Buddhahood.

Nichiren, for example, states: "The five characters Myoho-renge-kyo similarly reflect the ten thousand phenomena, not overlooking a single one of them.... A mirror that allows us to see our own image and reflection—such is Nam-myoho-renge-kyo" (OTT, 51–52). The "five characters Myoho-renge-kyo" and "Nam-myoho-renge-kyo" in this passage are synonymous with the Gohonzon, which embodies Nam-myoho-renge-kyo, or the essential Law of life and the universe.

A profound awareness that our lives are originally endowed with the Buddha's infinite wisdom and compassion is so crucial for our happiness that Nichiren goes so far as to say, "No other knowledge is purposeful" (WND, 299). The philosophical distance between Kierkegaard and Nichiren, therefore, is closer in their emphasis on self-knowledge than one might expect from their religious difference. The following are Kierkegaard's three requirements as applied to how we may better see ourselves in the mirror of the Gohonzon.

Why Don't We See Ourselves in the Mirror?

"The first requirement is that you must not look at the mirror, observe the mirror, but must see yourself in the mirror" (*For Self-Examination*, p. 25).

Here, Kierkegaard warns us against "the error of observing the mirror instead of seeing oneself in the mirror" (ibid., 25). One may ask how this could be possible. How can we look at the mirror and not see ourselves? Kierkegaard's first requirement, however, points to the subtlety of self-awareness.

Self-awareness is said to develop during the early years of life. In one psychological study, infants who had had a red spot applied to their nose were held up to a mirror. Those who recognized their own reflection and so reached for their own nose rather than the nose in the mirror were said to show at least some self-awareness. In this study, practically no infants in the first year of life showed clear evidence of self-awareness, whereas about 70 percent of infants between twenty-one and twenty-four months did so (see *Simply Psychology*, Michael W. Eysenck, p. 278).

Clearly those infants under one year observed the mirror but failed to see themselves. Their failure to see themselves in the mirror is their failure to connect what is reflected on the mirror to themselves. For those babies, the mirror served no purpose and became useless. This illustrates what essentially makes a mirror so valuable that we use it every day; it is our self-awareness or our ability to understand that what is reflected in the mirror is our own image.

Any adult of sound mind would not make the same mistake as those babies. When it comes to the Gohonzon, however, Kierkegaard's concern often becomes our reality. Although we revere the Gohonzon as Nichiren's enlightened life, we often fail to reflect the same respect back to our own lives. Or worse—some people may disparage their lives while admiring the Gohonzon's beneficial power. They might glorify the Gohonzon to the extent that they humble themselves. Still others may see the Gohonzon as life's mysterious truth beyond their grasp, accessible only for select priests.

Those who view the Gohonzon as an external deity or someone else's enlightenment may be compared to those infants reaching for the mirror instead of their own nose.

When we pray to the Gohonzon, we must reach into our own lives for the hidden gem of Buddhahood rather than reach out to the Gohonzon as an external source of salvation.

Our Invisible Self

"The second requirement is that in order to see yourself in the mirror...you must...remember to say to yourself incessantly: It is I to whom it is speaking; it is I about whom it is speaking" (*For Self-Examination*, p. 35).

Down the center of the Gohonzon is inscribed "Nam-myoho-renge-kyo Nichiren," indicating that the potential for absolute happiness exists within the lives of all people as represented by Nichiren, who was born to a fisherman's family, the lowest class in Japan's feudal society. So the Gohonzon speaks to each of us: "It is you who embodies the wonderful Law of Nam-myoho-renge-kyo just as Nichiren did!"

In this sense, our chanting of Nam-myoho-renge-kyo becomes our repeated affirmation of this message from the Gohonzon. As Kierkegaard's statement suggests, when we pray to the Gohonzon, we must remind ourselves that with each invocation we are manifesting our highest potential, full of strength and hope, no matter how our lives may appear on the surface.

Believing Is Seeing

"Finally, if you want to look at yourself in the mirror...you must not promptly forget how you looked" (ibid., 44).

Kierkegaard's final advice is his warning against our forgetfulness. When we study Nichiren's writings, we may intellectually understand that we are potentially Buddhas full of courage and compassion. While chanting, we may feel confident that our lives are essentially no different from that of Nichiren.

But minutes after we leave our homes for work or school, we often start acting in a manner unbefitting Buddhas. In the course of a day, we may also face one situation after another in which others disregard us as if we had not even an iota of Buddhahood.

This is why our consistent Buddhist practice and study become important as powerful reminders of our innate Buddhahood, especially when our environment seems to suggest its non-existence. Our diligent, conscious efforts steadily transform our intellectual idea of Buddhahood into our action as Buddhas and our fleeting awareness of Buddhahood into our unmovable conviction in the face of great hardship. In this sense, seeing ourselves in the Gohonzon is often a process of gradual transformation rather than an epiphany to attain once and for all.

Kierkegaard's vision of an ideal Christian was a "doer of the Word" (ibid., 25). To this end, he set down those three requirements for Christians to see themselves in the "mirror

of God's Word." By the same token, genuine Nichiren Buddhists must not simply be admirers of the Gohonzon who
see it with awe yet fail to see themselves in it. Indeed, what
those admirers think of as their pious respect for the
Gohonzon is a kind of fundamental disrespect that perverts
its purpose.

Nichiren wished us to become practitioners of the
Gohonzon who uphold this mirror of ultimate self-knowledge and appreciate our reflections. To this end, he stressed
the importance of faith, urging us "to summon up deep
faith that Myoho-renge-kyo is your life itself" (WND, 3). So
the true value of this wonderful mirror lies in the heart of
the beholder—the heart that knows believing is seeing.

(from the January 24, 2003, *World Tribune*)

FOOD FOR THOUGHT:

✦ Imagine what trouble could be caused if we believed that what is reflected in a mirror is not ours but someone else's reflection. What perspective allows us to actualize the value of the Gohonzon as the mirror of our innate Buddhahood? What misconception, on the other hand, could transform the Gohonzon into an instrument of confusion?

✦ Respect comes from understanding, but misunderstanding leads to disrespect. What are the right reasons for respecting the Gohonzon? What are the wrong reasons for respecting the Gohonzon?

KEY POINTS FOR CHAPTER 9

1) Arrogance results from our inclination to judge our self-worth by comparison with others. Genuinely confident people, on the other hand, are aware of their intrinsic personal strength or merit. The most reliable source of confidence is our innate Buddha nature.

2) Confidence makes genuine altruism possible. Confident people are free to care for others and fight for their happiness with the hope that it exceeds even their own.

3) The essential difference between arrogance and confidence is one of quality and origin. Arrogance is needy and dependent on others, derived from comparison with the external. Confidence is free and independent of others, found and cultivated in the self.

CHAPTER 9

Mistaking Arrogance for Confidence

NICHIREN DAISHONIN was often condemned by his contemporaries as "an extremely arrogant priest" for his confidence as a votary of the Lotus Sutra to "fulfill the Buddha's predictions and reveal the truth of his words" (WND, 400–01). Just as Nichiren's confidence was misconstrued as arrogance, we may be inclined to mistake our arrogance for confidence and others' confidence for arrogance. One of the five delusive inclinations, arrogance is considered in the Buddhist tradition both as a hindrance to enlightenment and as a cause for suffering. For this reason, mistaking arrogance for confidence is likely to set off a downward spiral of delusion and suffering. The fine line between arrogance and confidence, therefore, must be redrawn more clearly to distinguish happiness from delusion.

Judging One's Self-worth by Comparison With Others

The first of the seven types of arrogance, which are enumerated in some Buddhist scriptures, points to the essential quality of arrogance—"to think that one is superior to those inferior to oneself and that one is equal to one's equals" (*The Soka Gakkai Dictionary of Buddhism*, p. 579). Why is this arrogance? Isn't it just telling it like it is? What is implied here is that arrogance is essentially our inclination to judge our self-worth by comparing ourselves with others.

Certain comparisons between oneself and others may be objectively true—such as income, IQ or physical appearance. But to constantly judge one's self-worth through comparison with others in whatever standards chosen is to become arrogant. Of course, this is not to deny some merits that comparison and competition bring to our lives, such as motivation for improvement and an opportunity for self-reflection.

The correct assessment of our circumstances through comparison is essential to improving our lives. In fact, those living in isolation or unwilling to learn from others are arrogant. Comparison with others becomes a cause for concern when it becomes the sole measure for judging our existence. Put simply, if we start thinking of our lives as happy or unhappy, meaningful or meaningless, solely based on comparison with others, we may as well consider ourselves arrogant.

Arrogant people feel good about themselves only through affirming their superiority to others. Our sense of superiority is always relative to whomever we are compared with and never constant because of our changing circumstances. False confidence based on superiority, therefore, easily turns into a feeling of inferiority and self-disparage-ment, like a millionaire feeling poor among billionaires, a Ph.D. feeling foolish among Nobel laureates or a healthy person feeling overweight among supermodels. This is why false humility or self-disparagement is considered as arro-gance in Buddhism. (See the nine types of arrogance in *The Soka Gakkai Dictionary of Buddhism*, p. 457.) Put another way, arrogance and self-disparagement are two sides of the same coin; we cannot have one without the potential for the other.

Genuinely confident people, on the other hand, feel great about themselves without comparing themselves with oth-ers. Such people are aware of their intrinsic personal strength or merit worthy of praise and respect. Confident people can put into perspective their ups and downs of life. Their missed promotion or lost love does not spell out their failure as human beings. Their financial success or academic achievement does not necessarily make them superior to their peers. So long as they continue to be aware of their innate positive quality and strive to cultivate it, people will remain confident regardless of their external circum-stances. And Buddhism teaches that the most reliable source of confidence is our innate Buddha nature.

Arrogance Is Egotism, Confidence Is Altruism

What clearly distinguishes the arrogant from the confident is whether they desire and act for others' happiness greater than their own. Arrogant people are keenly aware that their self-esteem depends upon their superiority to others, so they often take delight in pitying the less fortunate since it reaffirms their superior status.

The "kindness" of the arrogant, however, extends only so far as it supports their self-importance; it continues as long as the less fortunate remain less fortunate. Precisely for this reason, the arrogant cannot desire and act for the supreme happiness of others because they fear it would diminish their own happiness. This explains why it is often easier to feel ambiguous pity for our underpaid coworkers than to share their joy over their sudden promotion. One's loss must be another's gain—this is the basic assumption of life held by the arrogant who cannot stop comparing their fortune with that of others.

Confidence, on the other hand, makes genuine altruism possible. Since confident people's self-worth does not depend upon others, they are free to care for others and fight for their happiness with the hope that it exceeds their own. In fact, the confident see their contribution to others' happiness as proof of their expanding humanity and as a source of great joy.

Confidence Is To Appreciate Oneself

In the late winter of 1272, Nichiren Daishonin wrote with his numbing hand: "I, Nichiren, am the richest man in all of present-day Japan. I have dedicated my life to the Lotus

Sutra, and my name will be handed down in ages to come"
(WND, 268).

A reformer who challenged the corrupt religious authority of his day, Nichiren was exiled, after a failed execution,
to a remote northern island of Japan, expected to die naturally or to be murdered. Destitute, he was living in a hut in a
field scattered with abandoned corpses, and everything
pointed to his approaching death.

These words, however, clearly express Nichiren's confidence that he gave his life to the spread of the essential
teaching of Buddhism, that is, the universality of Buddhahood. His life meant something for him, although it seemed
to have come to nothing. When he lost everything, he
gained the one thing that mattered most—indomitable
confidence that all people, no matter how miserable they
may appear, have the supreme potential of Buddhahood.

Through his own example, Nichiren demonstrated that
confidence need not depend on possessions or circumstances. Genuine confidence is to love and praise ourselves
even in the worst possible state, not for how we appear to
others but for what we are in the innermost of life.

The Arrogant Are Insecure and Needy

The difference between arrogance and confidence also
shows in our emotional state. Arrogance makes us insecure,
whereas confidence gives us peace of mind. The more arrogant we become, the more keenly we feel the dependence of

our happiness upon the misfortune and weakness of others.

This ironic dependence makes the seeming confidence of the arrogant increasingly insecure. The more they bolster this false self-confidence on the outside, the less secure they become inside; so the "happiness" of the arrogant is self-consuming.

As mentioned earlier, confident people are deeply aware that they derive their confidence from strengthening their innate qualities and need not depend on others. So the more confident people are, the more peaceful they will be with both themselves and others. Even in disagreement or when pointing out the errors of others, confident people can remain calm and open-minded. Since they need not defend their self-worth by "winning" the argument, confident people can stay focused on the merits of different views and opinions without becoming hurtful toward others.

Nichiren, for example, wrote from exile, "Whatever obstacles I might encounter, so long as persons of wisdom do not prove my teachings to be false, I will never yield!" (WND, 280). His vow to be steadfast in his belief comes with the condition—"so long as persons of wisdom do not prove my teachings to be false." This was an expression of the unruffled openness of the confident, not the blind obstinacy of the arrogant.

Think about how people behave at work. Unlike an arrogant manager who takes any suggestion as a personal criticism and everyone in the office as a potential threat, a confident manager takes even personal criticism as an opportunity for self-reflection and further improvement. The inner state of an arrogant person is constantly agitated, waiting for any opportunity to assert a sense of superiority. But the inner state of a confident person absorbs even an untoward event like a pebble tossed into a bathtub as opposed to a wineglass.

As it is clear now, arrogance is not too much confidence. The essential difference between arrogance and confidence is not one of quantity or degree but of quality and origin. Arrogance is needy and dependent on others, derived from comparison with the external. Confidence is free and independent of others, found and cultivated in the self.

Absolute Superiority Is a Dangerous Illusion

Mistaking arrogance for confidence distorts our view of humanity—the way we relate to others and ourselves. Such misconception spells out only tragic suffering for individuals and society. Long before his rise to power, Adolf Hitler wrote: "Self-confidence must be inculcated in the young national comrade from childhood on. His whole education and training must be so ordered as to give him the conviction that he is absolutely superior to others" (*Mein Kamph*, Ralph Manheim, trans., p. 411).

The epitome of arrogance, Hitler mistook the illusion of absolute superiority for supreme confidence. He debased education, turning it from a vehicle of equality and happiness into a cogwheel in the evil machinery of discrimination and destruction. Education must teach confidence, not arrogance. Likewise, Buddhist learning is to strengthen our faith in the inherent Buddha nature of others and ourselves, not to promote elitism among practitioners.

Nichiren was well aware of the danger of judging one's self-worth through comparison with others. He, therefore, admonished his disciples: "When you look at those of superior capacity, do not disparage yourself. The Buddha's true intention was that no one, even someone of inferior capacity, be denied enlightenment. Conversely, when you compare yourself with persons of inferior capacity, do not be arrogant and overproud. Even persons of superior capacity may be excluded from enlightenment if they do not devote themselves wholeheartedly" (WND, 62).

Here Nichiren explains that one's potential for enlightenment is in no way diminished by one's capacity to understand Buddhism since all people are equally endowed with supreme Buddhahood. What is most important for our happiness is to develop conviction in this intrinsic potential shared by all people. Our tendency to compare our capacity with that of others will only lead us astray from genuine happiness.

Nichiren, therefore, urges us to win over our arrogance in order to enjoy authentic happiness: "Now, if you wish to attain Buddhahood, you have only to lower the banner of your arrogance, cast aside the staff of your anger, and devote yourself exclusively to the one vehicle of the Lotus

Sutra" (WND, 58–59). Here, Nichiren indicates the close relationship between arrogance and anger. T'ien-t'ai, a sixth-century Chinese Buddhist scholar, described those in the state of anger as "always desiring to be superior to others" (GZ, 430). Anger is akin to arrogance; it may be described as frustrated arrogance.

As Nichiren suggests here, we can overcome our deep-seated arrogance and anger through our devotion to the "one vehicle of the Lotus Sutra"—that is, the teaching of the universality of Buddhahood and its essential practice as chanting Nam-myoho-renge-kyo. As we deepen our confidence in our own Buddhahood and this selfsame potential of others, the need to compare ourselves with others will diminish, and we will be free to appreciate and enjoy lives of our own making.

(from the March 7 and March 14, 2003, *World Tribune*)

FOOD FOR THOUGHT:

+ As seen in the example of Nichiren Daishonin, a confident person is often viewed as arrogant by those who are themselves arrogant. Why are the arrogant so disturbed by the confident?

+ In what way could the arrogance of the powerful be related to the despair of the powerless? How does the practice of Nichiren Buddhism help you develop genuine confidence when facing difficulties or feeling powerless?

+ How should we deal with people who display arrogant attitudes? Moreover, how can we use the practice of Nichiren Buddhism to self-reflect so that we ourselves may not mistake others' confidence for arrogance and our arrogance for confidence?

KEY POINTS FOR CHAPTER 10

1) Although the idea of creating peace by the use of force has been prevalent throughout history, force has consistently betrayed our expectation. An alternative for building substantial peace must be sought in an inner-directed spirituality.

2) Nichiren Buddhism offers a concrete means to achieve lasting peace through its teaching of Buddhahood's universality. Global peace comes about when people awaken to their shared goodness.

3) Prayer to affirm life's dignity and dialogue to promote mutual understanding are the key to overcoming the two major roadblocks to lasting peace—nationalism and fundamentalism.

CHAPTER 10

"Pax Humana" — Plan B for Peace

Nothing is more barbarous than war. Nothing is more cruel. And yet, the war dragged on. Nothing is more pitiful than a nation being swept along by fools.

—DAISAKU IKEDA, *THE HUMAN REVOLUTION*

WARS ARE USUALLY WAGED in the name of peace, for the sake of a nation. Our faith in force as an ultimate guarantor of peace has been robust since the ancient past, and in this cult of force, we keep going back to the fabled grandeur of Rome as a model of peaceful society achieved through the absolute superiority of military power. This vision of peace by force is called *pax Romana*, or Roman peace. The material foundation of *pax Romana* was a formidable institution of armed forces, and its spiritual mainstay the Roman virtue of *pietas*, that is, the citizens' selfless dedication to gods and the state. In the recent history of our nation, this vision of peace is also known as *pax Americana*.

The first Roman emperor Augustus brought peace and prosperity chiefly through the overwhelming strength of his army against "barbarians" such as the Celtic and Germanic peoples, whom the Romans thought of as moral and cultural inferiors, living both within and outside Rome's conquered territories. The popularity of Augustus's newly established imperial government was strong, as one historian wrote that he "conciliated...the world by the amenities of peace" (*Tacitus: The Histories and the Annals*, vol. 3, John Jackson, trans., p. 245). Virgil sang of Rome's divine mission to rule the world: "Roman, remember by your strength to rule / Earth's peoples—for your arts are to be these: / To pacify, to impose the rule of law, / To spare the conquered, battle down the proud" (*The Aeneid*, Robert Fitzgerald, trans., p. 190). *Pax Romana*, however, did not last long, nor were Rome's boundaries forever expansive. The empire gradually experienced more revolts in its provinces and invasions on its frontiers.

As deeply as faith in force has been rooted in our minds, force has consistently betrayed our expectation to create substantial peace. Although many emperors and kings, presidents and premiers, promised the sweetness of peace through the bitterness of war, they have not yet succeeded in the alchemy of transmuting fire and sword into the dove with an olive branch. This failure may be seen most recently in the rapid transitions from World War II into the Cold War, and from the Cold War into the global war on terrorism. While the technology of destruction has improved from rocks to rockets, from manpower to nuclear, the prospect of peace remains obscure, and the dividend of peace, however illusive and short-lived, has never been shared beyond the privileged citizens of powerful nations.

History only makes us wonder what new war will follow the end of the never-ending war on terrorism. After the long failure of force in achieving peace, it may be about time to question our faith in force and think about an alternative vision of peace.

"Reform the Tenets That You Hold in Your Heart"

Nothing is more precious than peace. Nothing brings more happiness. Peace is the most basic starting point for the advancement of humankind.
—*Daisaku Ikeda*, The New Human Revolution

In his treatise "On Establishing the Correct Teaching for the Peace of the Land," Nichiren Daishonin offers a "Plan B" for peace worth our serious consideration. Toward the end of this treatise, which takes the form of a dialogue between the host and his guest about how to create peace in a violent society, Nichiren writes in the voice of the host addressing his guest: "Therefore, you must quickly reform the tenets that you hold in your heart and embrace the one true vehicle, the single good doctrine [of the Lotus Sutra]. If you do so, then the threefold world will become the Buddha land, and how could a Buddha land ever decline?" (WND, 25).

Here "the single good doctrine of the Lotus Sutra" refers to the essential teaching of the Lotus Sutra, which is the universality of Buddhahood. This is the idea that all people—regardless of whatever differences they may have— share the supreme potential of Buddhahood, which is the source of universal virtues such as compassion and wisdom, hope and courage. In the treatise, Nichiren suggests that global peace comes about only when people awaken to their shared goodness.

Put simply, genuine peace is achieved essentially through individual inner transformation, not through change in government. This is a vision of peace radically different from our accustomed thinking. It is peace forged by faith in humanity, not faith in force; it is peace created by the awakened power of the powerless, not by the sanction and authority of government. This alternative for peace may well be called *pax humana*, or human peace.

In this regard, it is important to note that Nichiren's blueprint for peace is not based on religious sectarianism. As he later wrote, "I, Nichiren, am not the founder of any school, nor am I a latter-day follower of any older school" (WND, 669). For Nichiren, the universality of Buddhahood taught in the Lotus Sutra was the essential truth of life; it is the foundation upon which to build a global ethics that embraces the diversity of religion and race.

Also important to note is that Nichiren saw people at the center of nation-state, as indicated in his treatise, in which he often used the unusual Chinese character for nation by substituting one component signifying "king" with another signifying "people." Nichiren also addressed Hei no

Saemon, one of the most powerful government officials in his day, as "the arms and legs of all people" (GZ, 171). Central to Nichiren's vision of peace are individuals awakening to their shared goodness beyond the boundaries of religion and nation.

The Mind Without Borders

On February 17, 1952, second Soka Gakkai President Josei Toda addressed the youth after hearing their study presentations on Buddhism: "If I may express my own philosophy, mine is absolutely neither Communism nor Americanism; it is of the oriental race, and ultimately of the global race" (*Toda Josei Zenshu* [Collected Works of Josei Toda], vol. 3, p. 460). Amid the escalation of the Cold War and the deepening divisiveness in Asia, Toda reminded youth of the importance of transcending national boundaries first in their own hearts. Toda's idea of "the global race" points to the individual awakening of a shared humanity beyond race or nation, as envisioned by Nichiren.

Spreading its network of destruction from an Afghan cave to an Indonesian nightclub, terrorism is one of the global problems without borders, and as such it requires a mindset unrestricted by national boundaries. To transform our self-awareness into that of one global race, therefore, is crucial for the creation of international peace.

Two obstacles stand in the way of creating a global race: nationalism and fundamentalism. They are the malignant

outgrowths of what are ordinary human experiences: patriotism and faith. Patriotism turns into nationalism when it
asserts cohesiveness through hatred of other peoples and
draws fuel from a false sense of superiority. Faith turns into
fundamentalism when dogmas take precedence over human
happiness and the authority of priesthood mocks the prayer
of the desperate. When nationalism and fundamentalism
merge, the Orwellian nightmare becomes our daily reality:
"War is peace. Freedom is slavery. Ignorance is strength"
(George Orwell, *1984*, p. 3).

The spirit of Nichiren Buddhism, in one sense, is to
struggle against those two roadblocks to peace through the
power of prayer and dialogue. In his treatise on peace,
Nichiren writes, "If you care anything about your personal
security, you should first of all pray for order and tranquil-
ity throughout the four quarters of the land, should you
not?" (WND, 24). And he concludes the treatise with the
voice of the guest awakened to a new vision of peace, "We
must see to it that others as well are warned of their errors"
(WND, 26).

It may seem that peace through individual change is too
indirect and time-consuming to be effective in reality. But
once we as ordinary human beings renounce our faith in
force and start acting on this alternative vision of peace
through prayer and dialogue, we may be surprised by the
power of exponential expansion—as Nichiren wrote that
"two, three" awakened individuals are thereupon to be followed by "a hundred" (WND, 385).

As long as we continue to pray for and talk about the new vision of peace, the time will come sooner than we think when the heads of state must decide whether they listen to the voices of the new global race or become irrelevant to the course of human history.

(from the March 28, 2003, *World Tribune*)

FOOD FOR THOUGHT:

+ How can we utilize the practice of Nichiren Buddhism and SGI activities to achieve President Toda's vision for the "global race" in our daily lives, which often seem so removed from the rest of the world?

+ Faith in force is based on fear, and fear stems from a sense of powerlessness. What can we, as practitioners of Nichiren Buddhism, do to overcome irrational faith in force as an ultimate guarantor of peace?

+ No religion is immune to fundamentalism. From your own experiences, which humanistic aspect of Nichiren Buddhism is most effective to prevent a fundamentalist distortion of Buddhism?

KEY POINTS FOR CHAPTER 11

1) Internal corruption is religion's own poison; it needs to be recognized and kept under control, just as human evil can be checked but never eliminated. To acknowledge this is the first step religion must take if it wishes to remain true to its original intent.

2) In the story of Devadatta, Shakyamuni teaches that the antidote to religious corruption and authoritarianism is found in our wisdom and courage to perceive the truth and speak out against those of malicious intent.

3) We can develop the necessary wisdom and courage to challenge religious corruption by first looking inward and challenging our own Devadatta-like inclinations, such as arrogance and egotism.

CHAPTER 11

Denouncing Devadatta

W HAT SEEMS MOST UNBEFITTING of a Buddhist
is sometimes a most Buddhist thing to do under
certain circumstances—for example, denouncing
someone in public. What is known as "the act of information" during the Buddha's lifetime prompts us to rethink
our preconceived idea of what is appropriately Buddhist.

With his secret desire to gain control over the community of Buddhists, Devadatta, one of Shakyamuni's chief
disciples, urged his aged teacher to relinquish his responsibility and spend the rest of his life in leisure. Devadatta
made the proposal twice and was rejected. Devadatta then
asked Shakyamuni a third time in a public assembly: "Lord,
the Lord is now old, worn, stricken in years...It is I who will
lead the Order of monks" (*The Book of the Discipline: Vinaya-
Pitaka Cullavagga*, vol. 5, I. B. Horner, trans., p. 264).

Shakyamuni replied: "I...would not hand over the Order
of monks even to Sariputta and Moggallana. How then
could I to you, a wretched one to be vomited like spittle?"
(ibid., 264).

The Betrayal of Devadatta

Shakyamuni rebuked Devadatta as "spittle" because the latter was indulging himself with extravagant gifts and honors from a wealthy prince. Shakyamuni felt that Devadatta's attachment to fame and status should be pointed out in public. His arrogance and sense of superiority over other practitioners should be kept in check by comparing him with Shakyamuni's two other leading disciples. Instead, unaware that there was compassion behind his teacher's rebuke, Devadatta schemed to destroy the harmonious community of practitioners.

Sensing Devadatta's intention to cause a schism, Shakyamuni asked the whole Buddhist community to denounce Devadatta in the city of Rajagaha, informing believers and nonbelievers alike of Devadatta's corruption and betrayal: "Devadatta's nature was formerly of one kind, now it is of another kind" and "Whatever Devadatta should do by gesture and by voice, in that neither the Awakened One nor *dhamma* nor the Order should be seen, but in that only Devadatta should be seen" (ibid., 264–65). The Buddha declared, "Let the Order carry out a (formal) act of Information against Devadatta in Rajagaha" (p. 264).

Protecting the Buddhist Community

The leaders of the Buddhist community, however, were reluctant to publicly denounce Devadatta because they used to speak highly of him, praising his great ability and dignified appearance. Shakyamuni reminded his disciples that Devadatta's present evil was "just as true" as his past goodness (ibid., 265).

Overcoming their confusion and reluctance, the Buddhist leaders went out to denounce Devadatta. Townspeople responded differently to such unprecedented public denunciation against this famed leader of the Buddhist community, carried out by the Buddha's own disciples. Those of "little faith" and "poor intelligence" said, "They are jealous of Devadatta's gains and honours" (ibid., 266). But others who "had faith and were believing, who were wise, intelligent," said, "This can be no ordinary matter in that the Lord has Devadatta informed against in Rajagaha" (ibid., 266).

Thus begins the story of Devadatta's failed attempt to harm the Buddha and destroy the Buddhist community, as related in one of the early Buddhist scriptures. The purpose of the early Buddhists in recording these events is clear— they wanted to protect the community of practitioners upon which the integrity and spread of Buddhism depended. They were realists who knew that corruption and schism, which had occurred even during the Buddha's lifetime, were more likely to take place after the Buddha's passing.

Facing Internal Corruption

Religion must spread to continue its existence. But, to spread over different lands and through future generations, religion must be organized, however loosely or inconspicuously. Although some may find "organized" religion problematic, no religion can be completely devoid of organization or leadership. Otherwise, religion could not spread or even survive beyond a few generations.

With organization and leadership, however, come the elements of corruption. Authoritative leadership may turn authoritarian. Teachings to liberate believers from their suffering may be transformed into dogmas to keep them down. Responsibility and influence may attract those hungry for status and power. Shared resources may be abused to benefit a select few. For as long as organizations and their leadership are composed of human beings, it is not a matter of *if* they will be faced with corruption but *when*. Buddhism—as the episodes of Devadatta and many like him indicate throughout its long history—is no exception to this sober reality of religion.

Internal corruption is religion's own poison; it is religion's dormant cancer that needs to be kept under control, just as human evil can be checked but never eliminated. To acknowledge and face this fact is the first step religion must take; then it must develop an antidote against its own poison if it wishes to hold true to its noble, original intent.

In the story of Devadatta, Shakyamuni teaches us that the antidote to ensure the survival and integrity of Buddhism can be found in our wisdom and courage. Each member of the Buddhist community must develop the wisdom to perceive the truth beneath the surface and the courage to speak up against those of malicious intent, just like the Buddha's disciples did at the time of Devadatta's betrayal.

Although it should not be mistaken as license for emotional criticism or destructive slander, denouncing someone like Devadatta is our responsibility as Buddhists—an important way to repay our debt of gratitude owed to the precious community of practitioners.

We can develop the necessary wisdom and courage to carry out "the act of information" against Devadatta's kindred by first looking inward and challenging our own Devadatta-like inclinations such as arrogance and egotism. Only such honest self-reflection makes the act genuine and effective and prevents it from degenerating into ostracism.

(from the June 6, 2003, World Tribune)

FOOD FOR THOUGHT:

✦ Nichiren Daishonin speaks of those who, like Devadatta, attempted to destroy the unity of believers as follows: "Greedy, cowardly, and foolish, they nonetheless pass themselves off as wise persons" (WND, 800). How can we challenge such greed, cowardice, foolishness and hypocrisy that once in a while try to rear their ugly heads in our lives?

✦ In what sense is the public denouncement of Devadatta considered as Buddhist? Why is a failure to denounce evil considered as anti-Buddhist?

KEY POINTS FOR CHAPTER 12

1) In a society that fosters a sense of disconnection, Nichiren Buddhism sees our awareness of interconnectedness as a key to our genuine happiness. Nichiren Daishonin explains the importance of understanding the oneness of self and others—that our respect for others is essentially identical to our respect for ourselves.

2) The key to our personal well-being and the peace and harmony of the world lies in awakening ourselves from imaginary independence and reconnecting with the rest of humanity and the natural environment.

CHAPTER 12

An Illusion of Independence

THE WORLD AROUND US has become so interconnected that we find ourselves disconnected from it. The ever-increasing sophistication in commerce and communication makes it possible for us to go online and buy almost everything we want without ever stepping outside or meeting other people. Even when we go out to a supermarket, we are many steps removed by an intricate web of distribution from farmers and fishers. At a mall, we are thousands of miles away, across international borders, from those who actually made the shoes and clothes we're buying.

Disconnected From the Reality of Interdependence

Unlike medieval villagers who knew intimately where their bread and eggs came from, we never see those who make our lives possible, and we rarely think of them. Modern technology and the conveniences it brings have made us oblivious to how much our lives depend on the efforts of many others and the blessings of nature. We can survive on our own, it seems, as long as we have money. The interconnected world has made itself invisible to us, and the reality of complex interdependence has given way to an illusion of independence. We make our own living and buy what we want, so we are self-sufficient. In this way, we like to think of ourselves as independent.

Detachment, however, is not independence. Nor does our ignorance of interdependence make us self-sufficient. Such an illusion of independence is alarming because it carries the risk of giving people license to act without regard for others and the environment. To those who think that they are living on their own, the suffering of others and the destruction of nature become invisible. The only things that matter to them are themselves and what they own.

This is why it is not uncommon to see people who keep their own homes impeccably clean but nonchalantly litter the sidewalks or toss cigarette butts out their car windows. This is why some business and political leaders, who are likely loving and caring toward their own families, would not hesitate to exploit the poor of distant nations and destroy wildlife in need of preservation.

People's sense of self is made smaller by their illusion of independence. Their concept of self does not extend beyond the confines of their skin, their gene pools or the property lines around their homes. People's sense of community—that is, the feeling of "we" and "us"—often remains within their faiths or ideologies, lifestyle or income. The world has been increasingly divided into "self" and "other," into what is mine (which I must protect) and what is not mine (which I am free to exploit).

Expanding Our Awareness

Nichiren Buddhism sees our awareness of interconnectedness as a key to our genuine fulfillment. Nichiren Daishonin explains the importance of understanding the "fact that 'self' and 'others' are in fact not two different things" (OTT, 165). He points out that our respect for others is—in the innermost reality of life—identical to our respect for ourselves, just "like the situation when one faces a mirror and makes a bow of obeisance: the image in the mirror likewise makes a bow of obeisance to oneself" (OTT, 165).

Nichiren's message in this mirror analogy is clear. As long as we are caught up in the separation between self and other—thinking, "I will bow to you only if you bow to me first"—we will find ourselves in a frustrating waiting game that can lead to outbursts of anger and even violence. With each passing minute, we infuriate ourselves by misinterpreting the mirror's reflection of our frowns and glaring eyes as a personal insult inflicted upon us by others, who are unfortunately going through the selfsame process, trapped within the hard crust of their small ego.

The key to our personal well-being and the peace and harmony of the world then lies in awakening ourselves from the slumber of imaginary independence and reconnecting ourselves with the rest of humanity and the natural environment. There can be no true prosperity for humanity without conquering the disparity between the haves and the have-nots. There can be no lasting world peace without peace among peoples, without peace among religions. This seemingly overwhelming project can become a reality when we embrace the joys and sorrows of those around us and of those who, while separated from us by distance, are still deeply affected by our everyday actions and connected to us through our shared humanity. Expanding our awareness of what is required to succeed, in turn, begins with our daily Buddhist practice.

Can we develop our appreciation for those who make our lives possible and cultivate our sensitivity toward the natural world upon which our survival depends? Can we remove the spectacles colored by our attachment to religious differences and start seeing every person of every faith in the natural sunlight of humanity? Can we respect the planet's mountains, rivers and oceans as we would our own backyards? The globalization of business and technology will prove beneficial only if it keeps pace with the globalization of our mindset, with the expansion of our consciousness toward the global scale of nature and humanity.

(from the October 3, 2003, *World Tribune*)

FOOD FOR THOUGHT:

✦ Why are we so quick to draw lines—ethnic or religious, national or political—between "me" and "others," between "us" and "them"? What does becoming a global citizen mean to you?

✦ Has your Buddhist practice helped expand your awareness of interdependence or restored your connection with nature? If so, how?

KEY POINTS FOR CHAPTER 13

1) An important aspect of our Buddhist practice is to internalize the Buddhist teachings, digesting their meaning to our happiness and acting in accord with their intent. The main purpose of Buddhism is not to bind people with external precepts but to help them develop self-control and self-reliance, without which genuine freedom is impossible.

2) What appears Buddhist on the surface may not be truly Buddhist in substance. One who appears to be a teacher of Buddhism may be merely an imposter. In many of his writings, Nichiren Daishonin cautions us of our tendency to be caught up with people's appearance and lose sight of the substance and spirit of Buddhism.

Devadatta—The First Buddhist Fundamentalist?

DEVADATTA caused a schism that nearly destroyed the early Buddhist community. What can we learn from the greatest crisis of the Buddha's lifetime?

Typically, a fundamentalist movement is a reaction against the perceived threat of secularism, as in the conservative Protestant movements against evolutionary theories and liberal theology in the early twentieth century or today's various Islamic extremists against Western culture. The leaders of fundamentalist religions, therefore, often try to separate their followers from the rest of so-called corrupt society and unite them through distinct rules of behavior.

It is perhaps easier for many people to go along with rules, even those governing their most intimate choices regarding what to eat or whom to love, than to question the purpose of such rules. At the same time, there are many others who, even though they themselves cannot abide by such rules, admire others who live by or at least appear to live by them.

Devadatta's Scheme To Destroy the Buddhist Order

Devadatta—a prominent leader of the early Buddhist Order
who later betrayed his teacher—knew how to take advan-
tage of people's love of rules. After his failed attempts on
the Buddha's life (including sending assassins, hurtling a
boulder down on him and stampeding an elephant toward
him), Devadatta worked to create a schism in the Buddhist
Order by asking Shakyamuni to adopt five new rules that he
knew the Buddha would not accept.

According to the Vinaya-Pitaka, an early Buddhist text,
Devadatta's rules required members of the Order to: 1)
live in the forest and never go near a village; 2) beg for alms
and never accept invitations for meals; 3) wear robes made
of rags and never wear household robes; 4) sleep at the root
of a tree and never sleep under cover; and 5) never eat meat
and fish. Whoever in the Order failed to follow those rules,
Devadatta declared, "Sin would besmirch him" (*The Book of
the Discipline: Vinaya-Pitaka Cullavagga*, vol. 5, I. B. Horner,
trans., p. 276).

Devadatta then assured his cohorts of his plan's success:
"The recluse Gotama [Buddha] will not allow these. Then
we will win over the people by means of these five items. It
is possible...with these five items, to make a schism in the
recluse Gotama's Order, a breaking of the concord.
For...people esteem austerity" (ibid., 276).

As expected, the Buddha refused those rules, explaining
that it was up to each member how he would handle such

matters. Elated, Devadatta went to the city of Rajagriha and proudly announced, "The recluse Gotama does not allow these five items, but we live undertaking these five items" (ibid., 277). According to the Vinaya-Pitaka, those without faith and wisdom took the Buddha's response to mean he was in favor of seeking wealth. But those with faith and wisdom questioned Devadatta's motives: "How can this Devadatta go forward with a schism in the Lord's Order, with a breaking of the concord?" (ibid., 277).

When informed of the event, the Buddha explained that those who worked to destroy the Buddhist Order would suffer from "demerit that endures for an aeon" and those who challenged such attempts would enjoy "sublime merit...for an aeon" (ibid., 278). As a result of Devadatta's scheme, five hundred newer members deserted the Order. The Buddha then instructed Shariputra and Maudgalyayana, two of his trusted disciples, to help them understand the true teaching and return to the Order before they could "fall into trouble and distress" (ibid., 279).

The Buddha's Disciples Speak Out

When Shariputra and Maudgalyayana caught up with Devadatta's group, he was preaching to his new converts and assumed that those eminent disciples of the Buddha had come to join him. Despite a warning from his assistant Kokalika, Devadatta invited the pair to the assembly where he spoke to his followers until late into the night. Then, imitating the mannerisms of the Buddha, who was then past seventy, Devadatta said to his followers, "My back aches and I will stretch it" (ibid., 280). So saying, he quickly fell asleep.

Seizing the opportunity, Shariputra and Maudgalyayana eloquently explained the Buddha's true teachings, which dispelled the confusion of Devadatta's followers and led them all back to the Buddha. When Kokalika woke Devadatta, all his followers were gone. His shock was so great, it is said, that "at that very place hot blood issued from Devadatta's mouth" (ibid., 281).

Upon their return, the Buddha instructed Shariputra to be cautious about reinstating those who had left with Devadatta and to make them "confess a grave offence" (p. 282), perhaps to help them avoid making the same mistakes in the future.

When Shariputra reported how intently Devadatta was mimicking him, Shakyamuni warned his disciples of the foolishness of such behavior, comparing it to how young, ignorant elephants might mimic adult elephants eating lotus stalks but, by failing to clean them first, they become sick and die in agony. Then the Buddha predicted, "Devadatta will die, a wretched creature, copying me" (ibid., 282).

Seeing Through Imposters

This is the end of Devadatta's known history. The canonical texts do not tell his fate. According to one commentary, however, the earth opened up and swallowed him alive into hell. Did Devadatta's brand of strict asceticism survive? Fa-hsien, a fifth-century Chinese Buddhist pilgrim who traveled to India, reported in his *Travels* about a group in the Nepal area that had descended from Devadatta. Furthermore, in *The Record of the Western Regions of the Great T'ang Dynasty*, Hsüan-tsang, a seventh-century Chinese Buddhist translator known for his travels through Central Asia and India, recorded the existence of Devadatta's monastic community at Bengal. If these accounts are true, Devadatta's group survived some one thousand years after Shakyamuni's death, which is estimated to have occurred around either 480 or 380 BCE.

Devadatta might well qualify as the first Buddhist fundamentalist, a particularly malignant kind owing to his insincere advocacy of strict asceticism combined with blatant violence in usurping the leadership of the Buddhist Order. What is troubling about this early Buddhist episode is how easily so many members of the Order and Rajagriha citizens fell under Devadatta's influence, and how many centuries his influence might have lasted. Without the Buddha's penetrating insight into Devadatta's true nature and his disciples' courage, what might have happened to Buddhism?

Nichiren Daishonin admonishes our tendency to be deceived by imposters posing as true teachers: "Powerful enemies of the correct teaching...are to be found not so much among evil rulers and evil ministers, among non-Buddhists and devil kings, or among monks who disobey the precepts. Rather they are those great slanderers of the Law who are to be found among the eminent monks who appear to be upholders of the precepts and men of wisdom" (WND, 584).

Imposters are essentially concerned with the appearance of keeping precepts, while true practitioners question the relevance of precepts to the ultimate goal of Buddhist practice, that is, happiness for oneself and others. The purpose of a true practitioner is to internalize Buddhism and manifest it from deep within his or her life. One way not to be deceived by an imposter, then, is to embody the teachings of Buddhism instead of simply keeping up their appearance. That is, only when we practice true to the intent of Buddhism can we distinguish between *being* and *seeming*.

(from the February 13, 2004, *World Tribune*)

FOOD FOR THOUGHT:

+ What do you think it means to internalize the Buddhist teachings as opposed to merely imitating them? In terms of your own life, why is it important?

+ What is the difference between learning how to practice Buddhism from a mentor and imitating only the appearance of a mentor?

KEY POINTS FOR CHAPTER 14

1) We can respond to malicious lies causing
   mistrust and fear toward the community of
   Buddhist practitioners by verifying facts and
   communicating them clearly and widely.

2) The rhetoric of fear and mistrust has no effect
   on the secure and courageous. We ourselves
   must develop the courage to trust our innate
   Buddhahood and learn to live without fear.

The Spinning Club

ONCE IRRATIONAL MISTRUST and fear sink their dark roots in our minds, reason is often rendered powerless to uproot them. Mistrust turns truth into falsehood, and fear turns friends into foes. Suspicion seeks confirmation where there is none. Eventually, through the lens of mistrust and fear, insanity begins to appear as reason.

Perhaps this is why the sowing of mistrust and fear has been a well-used tool for those who thrive on manipulating others—from despots and demagogues to social climbers and insecure lovers. They spin half-truths and create a false image to incite mistrust and fear, like Iago turning Desdemona's handkerchief into a sign of infidelity for Othello. Thus, by the spinners of lies, the honest are turned into liars, and the naïve into accessories to crimes.

The Story of Sundari

In ancient India, as Shakyamuni's teachings spread and the Buddhist community grew, the leaders of other religious schools became jealous of Shakyamuni's success. So they accused the Buddha of sexual misconduct and violent crimes to discredit him and his movement.

Some of the early texts relate the story of Sundari. When Shakyamuni was staying in the city of Shravasti, his teachings quickly spread and his renown increased. But "wanderers belonging to other sects were not respected..., not honoured, being no gainers of robe, almsfood, lodging." They were "unable to endure the respect for the Lord [Shakyamuni]" (*The Udana*, Peter Masefield, trans., p. 74).

So they asked a woman called Sundari to frequent Jeta's Grove, where Shakyamuni was preaching. After making sure that many people saw her there, they had her killed and buried in the grove. Then they reported her missing to the king and requested him to check the grove. After the body was found, they took it to the streets, accusing the Buddha and his disciples of rape and murder, "How, indeed, could a man, having performed a man's duty, deprive the woman of her life?" (ibid., 75). The citizens harassed the Buddha's disciples as "those of poor morality, evil-natured, those telling lies" (ibid., 75).

Shakyamuni reassured his bewildered disciples that this calumny would not last long and encouraged them to challenge the allegation by reciting the following verse: "To hell shall go he that delights in lies, / And he who having done a thing, denies" (*The Jataka*, E. B. Cowell, ed., vol. 2, p. 284). Later, the ruffians who killed Sundari were caught, and they confessed who had hired them. The king ordered those behind the scheme to go round the city and declare:

"The guilt is not Gautama's, nor his disciples'; the guilt is ours!" (ibid., 284).

The Story of Chincha

Another text tells the story of Chincha. When Shakyamuni was staying in the same city, the leaders of other religious schools conspired, "How can we cast a stain upon Gautama...in the face of men, and put an end to his honour and his gifts?" (*The Jataka*, E. B. Cowell, ed., vol. 4, p. 116). They asked beautiful Chincha to destroy Shakyamuni's reputation.

Dressed up and perfumed, Chincha would go toward Jeta's Grove as the citizens were leaving after hearing the Buddha's preaching. She would then spend the night nearby and go toward the city in the morning as the citizens approached the grove. When anyone asked what she was doing, she would reply, "What have you to do with my goings and comings?" (ibid., 116). But after some six weeks, she declared, "I spent the night...with Gautama [Shakyamuni]" (ibid., 116). Thus the rumor began.

After eight or nine months, she tied a bundle of wood under her robe to look pregnant and beat her hands and feet to look swollen. She then went to a public assembly where Shakyamuni was preaching and said: "You preach indeed to great multitudes; sweet is your voice, and soft is the lip that covers your teeth; but you have got me with child, and my time is near; yet you assign me no chamber for the childbirth.... You know how to take your pleasure, but you do not know how to care for that which shall be born!" (ibid., 117).

Shakyamuni stopped his talk and replied, "Whether that which you have said be true or false, you know and I know only" (ibid., 117).

"Yes, truly," said Chincha, "this happened through something that you and I only know of" (ibid., 117).

At that moment, the god Shakra and his retinue came in the form of mice and gnawed through the cords, and the bundle of wood fell at her feet.

In the story of Sundari, Shakyamuni urged his disciples to speak up against the groundless accusations, and with the arrest of those responsible, the rumor disappeared. In the story of Chincha, the truth of the matter was revealed by divine intervention—*deus ex machina*. But this incident, so skillfully planned, must have been confusing to many. One may wonder what those little mice represented. Inspired by a sense of justice, some nameless disciples might have taken it upon themselves to disclose the machinations of those harboring jealousy and hatred toward the Buddhist community.

Challenging Lies and Liars

The distasteful nature of these events and the fact that they are recounted in various Buddhist texts, both early and late, speak to the likelihood that these were actual occurrences and not mere allegory. In any case, both stories tell the importance of challenging lies and revealing truths.

Centuries later, subjected to similar accusations, Nichiren Daishonin writes: "Though I have neither wife nor child, I am known throughout the country as a monk who transgresses the code of conduct, and though I have never killed even a single ant or mole cricket, my bad reputation has spread throughout the realm. This may well resemble the situation of Shakyamuni Buddha, who was slandered by a multitude of non-Buddhists during his lifetime" (WND, 42). Nichiren also warned his disciples: "Those who believe in the Lotus Sutra should beware of and guard themselves against the sutra's enemies.... If you do not know your enemies, you will be deceived by them" (WND, 664).

In a broader sense, these "enemies" of the Lotus Sutra may include those who spread lies about the community of practitioners dedicated to the sutra's essential message, that is, respect for all life.

Once, the Soka Gakkai was labeled as a "gathering of the sick and poor." Now the media, especially in Japan, sometimes describe—whether intentionally or out of ignorance—our growing international movement as "powerful" or "potentially dangerous." Regarding those negative images created by the media then and now, SGI President Ikeda writes: "While these labels express opposite extremes, they share a common attitude of disdain for the people. This probably points to a feeling of resistance toward, and envy of, ordinary people becoming independent, raising their voices, and playing a decisive role in society" (May 1003 *Living Buddhism*, p. 24).

How then can we respond to malicious lies causing mistrust and fear toward the community of practitioners? First, by verifying facts and communicating them clearly and widely. Today this task is both facilitated and frustrated by mass media and the Internet. Facts alone, however, cannot effectively dispel mistrust and fear. More fundamentally, we ourselves must develop the courage to trust our innate Buddhahood and learn to live without fear. The rhetoric of fear and mistrust has no effect on the secure and courageous.

(from the May 14, 2004, *World Tribune*)

FOOD FOR THOUGHT:

✦ Have you had a breakthrough, based on your Buddhist practice, with someone who tried to manipulate you with fear and mistrust?

✦ How would you respond to false reports by the media about our faith community? How can each of us become a better spokesperson for Nichiren Buddhism?

KEY POINTS FOR CHAPTER 15

1) Authoritarianism thrives on blind obedience, which spreads in any society or organization where people view themselves as a means to an end and seek to escape personal responsibility for their actions.

2) Nichiren Buddhism revives the Buddhist tradition that the correctness of one's action based on life's truth stands above both secular and religious authority.

3) To prevent blind obedience, we must develop the courage to accept personal responsibility for our action and learn that no person should be treated as a means to an end because each person is worthy of utmost respect for his or her innate Buddhahood.

CHAPTER 15

On Blind Obedience

OBEDIENCE TO AUTHORITY may be deemed as a virtue when authority represents truth and good will. Obedience becomes a catalyst for horrendous suffering, however, when authority represents untruth and malice. For this reason, blind obedience—that is, obedience without moral judgment—is the foremost companion sought after by those perpetrating evil.

The Dangers of Blind Obedience

Social psychologist Stanley Milgram observes, "The essence of obedience consists in the fact that a person comes to view himself as the instrument for carrying out another person's wishes, and he therefore no longer regards himself as responsible for his actions" (*Obedience to Authority*, p. xii). Malicious authority thrives in any society or organization where people view themselves as a means to an end and seek to escape personal responsibility for their actions.

Originally, Buddhism stressed the dangers of blind obedience. Buddhism placed the correctness of one's action above both secular and religious authority. Early Buddhists, as one Buddhist scholar points out, believed that justice must be upheld above the authority of nations and kings; they challenged the religious circle of the day by asserting that truth transcends even the authority of gods (see Hajime Nakamura, *Nakamura Hajime senshu* [The Selected Works of Hajime Nakamura], vol. 17, pp. 40–42). This is exemplified in an early Buddhist text where Shariputra, one of Shakyamuni's main disciples, tells a negligent Brahman that one who acts justly is better than one who acts unjustly "for the sake of the king" or "for the sake of the deities" (*The Middle Length Discourses of the Buddha*, p. 793).

Nichiren's Spiritual Independence

After more than a millennium of dogmatism and authoritarianism had overshadowed Buddhist history, Nichiren Daishonin revived the original spirit of Buddhism. In 1271, amid the crowd of warriors on his way to the execution site, Nichiren rebuked the guardian deity of Japan's warrior class for failing to "protect the votary of the Lotus Sutra" (WND, 767). He called out to the god, "Great Bodhisattva Hachiman, are you truly a god?" (WND, 766).

Nichiren thought that what he called the "mystic truth that is originally inherent in all living beings" (WND, 2) and those who spread this truth of life must be placed above the authority of gods and deities, not to mention the authority of priests.

The execution attempt failed, and Nichiren was exiled to a remote northern island. When he returned from his exile in 1274, he met one of the most powerful government officials. At this meeting, he declared his belief that life's supreme truth surpasses the secular authority: "Even if it seems that, because I was born in the ruler's domain, I follow him in my actions, I will never follow him in my heart" (WND, 579). Nichiren refused to become an instrument of religious or secular authority, followed his conscience and embraced the consequences of his action with joy. In so doing, he experienced an immense sense of freedom in his exile.

Upholding the Truth of Life

The truth of life must be upheld above the authority of kings and gods—such thinking is still as revolutionary today as it was in ancient India. Today, as well as in the past, life's dignity, truth and justice are often invoked only when they seem to support national interests or religious dogmas. Rarely have we seen nations or religions willing to compromise on their interests and dogmas for the sake of universal values that transcend the boundaries of nations and faiths.

The early Buddhist anti-authoritarian stance encourages modern Buddhists to be aware of the pitfall of dogmatism. Do Buddhists say, "It's true because the Buddha says so"? Or do they say, "The Buddha says so because it's true"?

The warning of the early Buddhists also applies to the members of any society. Do the citizens of a republic say, "It's true because the government says so"? Or do they seek the truth of a matter and then judge the actions of the government?

The universal truth of life comes before religions and nations. Blind obedience to authority—whether it is religious or political—not only obscures life's truth but also causes enormous suffering, as the history of humanity has repeatedly shown us through persecutions and genocides. People are not a means to an end. Each person is responsible for his or her actions. To learn these simple lessons, one must first discover the infinite value in each life and develop the courage to accept personal responsibility—that is, the joyful burden of freedom.

(from the Januray 14, 2005, *World Tribune*)

FOOD FOR THOUGHT:

✦ "People are not a means to an end"—what does this statement mean to you? Why do some people wish to become the instruments for carrying out others' wishes rather than the actors of their own will?

✦ In your opinion, why did Nichiren Daishonin experience an immense sense of freedom when he was exiled? What do you think is the key to living true to yourself, especially in a time of hardship?

KEY POINTS FOR CHAPTER 16

1) Good and evil are innate, inseparable aspects of life. This Buddhist concept of the oneness of good and evil, however, does not mean that evil is good, nor does it imply that the distinction between good and evil is irrelevant. Instead, it teaches us to perceive and triumph over evil through faith in the universal goodness of life.

2) The faith that enables us to experience the freedom and happiness of Buddhahood is synonymous with the courage to see our potential for both good and evil. The process of accepting and challenging our fundamental darkness is necessarily the process of revealing our innate enlightenment.

CHAPTER 16

The Courage To Accept Our Innate Good and Evil

THE EVIL OF DESTRUCTION is like a shadow cast by the good of creation. Nature gives and takes life. Even on the cellular level of the human body, the evil of decay and death exists side by side with the good of growth and health.

For example, while the precise mechanism of cancer remains unknown, research has demonstrated that the malignant transformation of a cell is linked to cancer-causing genes called oncogenes. In normal cells, oncogenes are called proto-oncogenes, which promote cellular growth and are regulated by cellular genes called tumor-suppressor genes. Tumor-suppressor genes, in other words, control growth-promoting genes, which could potentially turn malignant. (see "Cancer: Causation." "The Cause of Disease: Abnormal Growth of Cells." *Encyclopaedia Britannica*, CD-ROM, 1999). Thus, the potential for cancer not only exists in every cell of the body, but also supports the cell's growth and health.

Life's Innate Good and Evil

Concerning the nature of good and evil, Nichiren Daishonin writes: "Good and evil have been inherent in life since
time without beginning…. The heart of the Lotus school is
the doctrine of three thousand realms in a single moment of
life, which reveals that both good and evil are inherent even
in those at the highest stage of perfect enlightenment. The
fundamental nature of enlightenment manifests itself as
Brahma and Shakra, whereas the fundamental darkness
manifests itself as the devil king of the sixth heaven" (WND,
1113). Nichiren explains that all people are endowed with
supreme good and evil, as well as all the possible life-states
in between. We can be either as godly as "Brahma and
Shakra" or as devilish as the "devil king."

Good and evil, in other words, are innate, inseparable
aspects of life. This Buddhist concept is called the "oneness
of good and evil." This teaching, however, does not mean
that evil is good, nor does it imply that the distinction
between good and evil is irrelevant. Instead, it teaches us to
perceive and triumph over evil inside—thereby conquering
evil on the outside—through confidence in the universal
goodness of life.

In the context of Nichiren's teaching, good means the
"fundamental nature of enlightenment," or absolute freedom and happiness resulting from profound self-knowledge. Evil indicates the "fundamental darkness," or life's
innate delusion negating the potential of enlightenment

and causing suffering for oneself and others. This inner darkness echoes with the despair that our lives are ugly and meaningless; it drives a wedge of fear that splits the hearts of people into "us" and "them." Nichiren's concept of good and evil, in this sense, may be better understood as the dynamic, innate workings of life that become manifest or dormant, rather than the external moral codes determined by cultural and social conditions.

Understanding the Oneness of Good and Evil

A Buddha is someone who has the courage to acknowledge those two fundamental aspects of life. As Nichiren writes, "One who is thoroughly awakened to the nature of good and evil from their roots to their branches and leaves is called a Buddha" (WND, 1121). Buddhas accept their innate goodness without arrogance because they know all people share the same Buddha nature. Buddhas also recognize their innate evil without despair because they know they have the strength to overcome and control their negativity.

Buddhas understand the hearts of people in myriad conditions and circumstances. Buddhas are capable of guiding others to their own awakening. This is because Buddhas share the same conditions as others, yet have the strength and wisdom to control their own evil.

Much of our difficulty in discerning the workings of good and evil is due to our unwillingness to acknowledge the potential of both supreme good and evil within our own lives. We don't want to see ourselves as either very good or very bad, hiding instead behind a collective moral mediocrity that requires neither the responsibility of goodness nor the guilt of evil. To flee from the responsibility to realize the full potential of our innate goodness, we say, "I can't be as good as...." To avoid a sense of guilt, we say, "I can't be as bad as...." (Fill in the blanks with the names of those whom you think supremely good and bad respectively, or "Buddha" in the former blank and "devil" in the latter.)

For some of us, our moral ambiguity of the self, however, seems to demand quick judgment of others—those who serve our interest as "good people" and those whom we dislike as "bad people"—as if to counterbalance our inner confusion with our forced clarity outside. Others seem unable to denounce the clearly manifest evil of humanity for fear of being judged in return. Such people fear the judgment of others because they themselves lack the courage to see their own potential for good and evil. As a result, our view of the world becomes narrow if not distorted.

Challenging Evil Within

Paul Tillich, a noted philosopher and theologian of the last century, said, "The courage to affirm oneself must include the courage to affirm one's own demonic depth" (*The Courage to Be*, p. 122).

In the same regard, Carl Jung said, "Everyone carries a

shadow, and the less it is embodied in the individual's con-scious life, the blacker and denser it is" (*Psychology and Religion*, p. 93). Jung also made the following observation of a person who develops the courage to face the potential of evil within: "Such a man knows that whatever is wrong in the world is in himself, and if he only learns to deal with his own shadow then he has done something real for the world" (ibid., 101–02).

Nichiren had the courage to see his own "demonic depth," as he candidly writes: "Although I, Nichiren, am not a man of wisdom, the devil king of the sixth heaven has attempted to take possession of my body. But I have for some time been taking such great care that he now no longer comes near me" (WND, 310). Nichiren had the courage to see his own fundamental darkness. In spite of this sober reality, he summoned forth confidence in his innate Buddhahood and thus overcame life's tendency to deny its own highest reality. As he states, "The single word 'belief' is the sharp sword with which one confronts and overcomes fundamental darkness or ignorance" (OTT, 119–20).

The faith that enables us to experience the freedom and happiness of Buddhahood is synonymous with the courage to see our potential for both good and evil. The process of accepting and challenging our fundamental darkness is necessarily the process of revealing our innate enlightenment. Likewise, our efforts to help others become aware of their own self-negating delusion must be accompanied by our efforts to help them become aware of their own self-affirming power of enlightenment. Without one, the other is impossible.

To see our innate good and evil is to experience the joy of accepting our whole being. As Tillich said, "Joy is the emotional expression of the courageous Yes to one's own true being" (*The Courage to Be*, p. 14). Such honest and courageous acceptance of the self also marks the beginning of the essential transformation of our lives and the world around us.

(from the February 2002 *Living Buddhism*)

FOOD FOR THOUGHT:

✦ Why is courage necessary in order to recognize our potential for good and evil? What do you think is the benefit of recognizing not only goodness but evil innate within our lives?

✦ What is the significance of the Buddhist concept of the oneness of good and evil in terms of our Buddhist practice and daily life?

Key Points for Chapter 17

1) The historical origin of the Buddha nature concept may be traced back to the early Buddhist concept of the "luminous mind." Early Buddhists thought that people are endowed with the pure mind, but it is covered with delusions.

2) The Lotus Sutra stresses the universality of Buddhahood by recognizing its potential in those denied enlightenment in other Buddhist teachings. The tradition of the Buddha nature concept teaches that we must challenge our delusions to reveal our Buddha nature.

3) Nichiren Daishonin teaches that when we chant Nam-myoho-renge-kyo, we are praising the Buddha nature of all living beings and, at the same time, bringing forth this supreme potential of life from within our own lives. The key to manifesting our Buddha nature lies in our confidence in its existence.

CHAPTER 17

Freeing the Caged Bird Within

ONE WORD sometimes makes a world of difference. When the practitioners of Mahayana Buddhism—the popular, altruistic Buddhist movement that arose around the first century of the Common Era partly in reaction to the ascetic traditions of earlier Buddhism—added the word *nature* to the word *Buddha*, this newly coined term caused a radical transformation of how Buddhism was viewed and practiced, especially in East Asian countries such as China and Japan.

Buddhism was the sacred teaching taught by the Buddha, but with the development of the Buddha nature concept, it also came to be understood as the "Buddha vehicle"—that is, the teaching by which to become a Buddha.

The Buddha nature refers to the potential for attaining Buddhahood, a state of awakening filled with compassion and wisdom. Although the Buddha nature and Buddhahood are sometimes used interchangeably, strictly speaking, the Buddha nature is one's potential for becoming a Buddha, and Buddhahood is the manifest state of that potential. Through the development of the Buddha nature concept, Buddhahood became the universal principle of authentic happiness rather than the isolated awakening of one gifted person.

The Origins of the Buddha Nature

The Buddha nature concept is a characteristic teaching of Mahayana Buddhism, but its origin can be traced back to early Buddhism. In an early scripture, for example, Shakyamuni talks about the "luminous mind" (Skt *citta-prakrti*) covered by the layers of delusion: "This mind...is luminous, but it is defiled by taints that come from without; that mind...is luminous, but it is cleansed of taints that come from without" (*The Book of the Gradual Sayings*, trans. F. L. Woodward, vol. 1, pp. 7–8).

Shakyamuni explains that since people are unaware of their innate luminous mind, they do not even try to cultivate their potential. So the brilliance of this luminous mind remains obscured.

After Shakyamuni's death, the early Buddhists strove to achieve the state of *arhat*, or "worthy one," by following his teachings. *Arhat* was originally synonymous with Buddha, or "awakened one." Later, however, it became distinguished from Buddha. While the practitioners of the ascetic traditions sought the state of *arhat* as their highest attainment, the state of Buddhahood was reserved exclusively for Shakyamuni.

Meanwhile, after Shakyamuni's death, ordinary people—who could not afford to study and practice Buddhism as rigorously as did monks—tried to ease their anxiety about the general belief that the great Buddha, having extinguished his flame of selfish cravings, put an end to the cycle of reincarnation and would never be reborn in this world. If so, what would happen to those left behind? They responded to their spiritual crisis in two ways: one was to seek salvation outside; the other was to seek the potential of salvation within. Those two ideas, salvation from outside and within, developed gradually in the Mahayana tradition—sometimes together, sometimes separately.

Since the essence of Shakyamuni's enlightenment is the universal truth of liberation, people reasoned there must be more than one Buddha existing throughout time and space eager to help them. Thus was born the idea of a savior Buddha who remains in this universe to continually save the people from suffering—such as Amitabha and Vairochana as Buddhas of the present, and Maitreya as a future Buddha. People also felt that the Buddha tried to save all people from suffering because he saw that they already had some internal cause or potential to attain Buddhahood. This eventually gave rise to the Buddha nature concept of Mahayana Buddhism.

For example, the Flower Garland Sutra (likely compiled before the year 200) describes the neglected existence of the Buddha wisdom in all living beings. It states: "There is not a single sentient being who is not fully endowed with the knowledge of Buddha; it is just that because of deluded notions, erroneous thinking, and attachments, they are unable to realize it. If they would get rid of deluded notions, then universal knowledge, spontaneous knowledge, and unobstructed knowledge would become manifest" (*The Flower Ornament Scripture*, Thomas Cleary, trans., p. 1002).

But of all the early Mahayana scriptures, the Lotus Sutra stands out in terms of representing the view of salvation from within. The Lotus Sutra—part of which possibly dates from the first century BCE— repeatedly emphasizes the universality of Buddhahood. For example, it states, "If there are those who hear the Law, / then not a one will fail to attain Buddhahood" (LS, 41). It also states, "The original vow of the Buddhas / was that the Buddha way, which they themselves practice, / should be shared universally among living beings / so that they too may attain this same way" (LS, 41).

The Lotus Sutra stresses the universality of Buddhahood by recognizing its potential in those denied enlightenment in other Buddhist teachings. For example, many Mahayana sutras asserted that monastics and solitary mendicants were incapable of attaining Buddhahood. Incapable as well, in some Buddhist traditions, were women and evil men. The Lotus Sutra, however, recognizes the potential for Buddhahood in all categories of people denied enlightenment elsewhere.

Another important feature of the Lotus Sutra is that all people are acknowledged as the children of the Buddha. The Buddha's disciples proclaim: "So we did not know that we were in truth the sons of the Buddha. But now at last we know it" (LS, 86). The sutra also explains, "And if in future existences / one can read and uphold this sutra, / he will be a true son of the Buddha" (LS, 181). All people, the sutra teaches, are related to Shakyamuni—that is, they share the Buddha's spiritual makeup and therefore will eventually develop into Buddhas, just as a child inevitably grows into an adult.

From the Baby Buddha to the Buddha Nature

By the mid-third century, Mahayana Buddhists in India came up with a new term for people's Buddha potential— *tathagatagarbha*. *Tathagata* means either the "one who has gone [to the realm of truth]" or the "one who has come [from the realm of truth]." This is another name for a Buddha. *Garbha* means the womb and, by extension, the embryo or fetus. The concept of *tathagatagarbha*, therefore, signifies that the people are "baby Buddhas" who—with proper care and cultivation—will eventually grow into full-fledged Buddhas.

The Shrimala Sutra—dating from the mid-fourth century—explains the permanently unchanging nature of *tathagatagarba*. "The Tathagatagarbha is not born, does not die, does not pass away to become reborn....The Tathagata-garbha is permanent, steadfast, eternal" (*The Lion's Roar of Queen Srimala*, Alex and Hideko Wayman, trans., pp. 104–05). But the same sutra cautions that *tathagatagarbha* should not be mistaken for the unchanging existence of the self that the Buddhist tradition has long denied. "The Tathagatagarbha is neither self nor sentient being, nor soul, nor personality" (ibid., 106). This sutra emphasizes that "only through faith in the Tathagata" can one understand how the intrinsically pure potential for Buddhahood exists in a defiled condition (ibid., 107).

It is the Nirvana Sutra that uses the expression "Buddha nature" for the first time. The lost Sanskrit original of this sutra was compiled probably around 300–350. Extant Chinese translations were produced around 420. This sutra repeatedly proclaims that all living beings possess the Buddha nature. The original Sanskrit term for the Buddha nature is thought to be *buddhadhatu* ("Buddha's foundation or essence") or *buddhagotra* ("Buddha's lineage"), signifying the potential for attaining Buddhahood as well as the proof that all people can grow into Buddhas. The sutra's conviction is expressed through the Buddha's proclamation: "I roar like a lion that all living beings definitely possess the Buddha nature" (translation based on *Kokuyaku issaikyo indo senjutsubu nehanbu*, vol. 2, p. 458 and *Budda rinju no seppo*, vol. 3, p. 262).

The Buddha Nature Is Like Yogurt

The author of the Nirvana Sutra was acutely aware of his critics. The sutra claims that all people possess this magnificent true self of the Buddha nature. But how is this different from the illusion of unchanging selfhood that Buddhism has long warned people against? Our lives change constantly through causes and conditions, and nothing remains the same.

The Nirvana Sutra teaches that despite the impermanence of all phenomena, each person's life has the unchanging potential of genuine happiness. This potential, or Buddha nature, is beyond the conception of existence or nonexistence and will become manifest through one's correct Buddhist practice. Without such cultivation, however, the Buddha nature seems not to exist at all in our lives.

In the Nirvana Sutra, the Buddha explains this peculiar characteristic of the Buddha nature through the metaphor of yogurt and milk. The Buddha nature is like yogurt, the Buddha teaches. And people's lives are like milk. The Buddha explains: "You must not say with certainty either that yogurt exists in milk or that yogurt does not exist in milk. Nor should you say that it arises from something else" (translation based on *Kokuyaku issaikyo indo senjutsubu nehanbu*, vol. 1, p. 150, and *Budda rinju no seppo*, vol. 1, p. 287).

From one point of view, we can say that people have the Buddha nature because Buddhas are nothing other than people in flesh and blood. So the Buddha teaches, "I say that yogurt exists [in milk] because it comes from milk" (translation based on *Kokuyaku issaikyo indo senjutsubu nehanbu*, vol. 2, p. 485, and *Budda rinju no seppo*, vol. 3, p. 313). From another point of view, we cannot say that people have the Buddha nature when they are deluded about their true potential. So the Buddha asks his disciple, "If yogurt exists in milk as you say, why does the milk seller accept only the price of milk and does not ask for the price of yogurt?" (translation based on *Kokuyaku issaikyo indo senjutsubu nehan-bu*, vol. 2, p. 487, and *Budda rinju no seppo*, vol. 3, p. 316).

All people, the Nirvana Sutra teaches, have the Buddha nature. But this assurance of the immanence of Buddhahood still requires us to cultivate this potential— unrealized potential is as good as nothing.

Discovering the Buddha Nature

It takes resolute courage to believe in the Buddha nature dormant beneath our layers of delusion. Only by believing that it exists, however, can we begin the wonderful journey of self-discovery. Believing in our innate Buddha nature is difficult—especially when our past experience tells us that we are unworthy of happiness, when our present circumstances tell us that despair is the only choice. Even when things are going well, we may think, *Who needs this Buddha nature anyway?*

Perhaps it is for those who stubbornly refuse to believe in the Buddha nature that ancient Buddhist teachers came up with so many analogies to teach the importance of faith in this most wonderful potential of life.

The Tathagatagarbha Sutra, for example, is a repository of fine metaphors for the innate Buddha nature hidden beneath our delusions. For example, the Buddha proclaims:

"When I regard all beings with my buddha eye, I see that hidden within the *klesas* [delusions] of greed, desire, anger, and stupidity there is seated augustly and unmovingly the *tathagata*'s wisdom, the *tathagata*'s vision, and the *tathagata*'s body. Good sons, all beings, though they find themselves with all sorts of *klesas*, have a *tathagatagarbha* [the Buddha nature] that is eternally unsullied, and that is replete with virtues no different from my own" ("The Tathagatagarbha Sutra," William H. Grosnick, trans., *Buddhism in Practice*, Donald S. Lopez, ed., p. 96).

Furthermore, the sutra claims that the Buddha nature in all living beings is a fact of life, regardless of whether the Buddha teaches of its existence: "Whether or not buddhas appear in the world, the *tathagatagarbhas* of all beings are eternal and unchanging. It is just that they are covered by sentient beings' *klesas*" (ibid., 96).

The noteworthy Tathagatagarbha Sutra metaphors for the Buddha nature include describing it as pure honey surrounded by a swarm of angry bees (ibid., 97). The Buddha skillfully removes the angry bees—that is, delusions—and then shares the honey with many people, encouraging them to enjoy the pure honey within their own lives. Sometimes, people do feel as if covered with angry bees ready to sting, especially when they try to reach into the happier part of their lives. Through our Buddhist practice, however, we can develop the wisdom to calm and control our destructive impulses, and this process of challenging our dark desires is in itself the process of revealing our innate Buddha nature.

The Tathagatagarbha Sutra also compares the Buddha nature to a kernel of wheat in a husk (ibid., 97–98). A poor, hungry person discards wheat, thinking it useless because it is covered with prickly husks he cannot eat. So the Buddha teaches: "But although the outside seems like something useless, / The inside is genuine and not to be destroyed. / After the husks are removed, / It becomes food fit for a king" (ibid., 97–98). Again, the removal of the husk of negativities is in itself the revelation of the Buddha nature kernel. Do not judge your life as useless, the Buddha teaches here, merely by its appearance.

Other metaphors of the Buddha nature in this sutra include the finding of pure gold in a pit of excrement (ibid., 98). This metaphor emphasizes the unchanging value of the Buddha nature and that this "pure gold" is to be found in the place least expected, the trouble-ridden lives of ordinary people.

The sutra also depicts the Buddha teaching: "[The Buddha nature] is just like the pit of a mango fruit / Which does not decay. / Plant it in the earth / And inevitably a great tree grows" (ibid., 99–100). This metaphor underscores the importance of cultivating the Buddha nature through Buddhist practice as well as of recognizing life's greatest potential despite surface appearances. With a tree more familiar to those living in North America, this analogy may be rephrased as the following: instead of judging the little, mud-covered acorn by its appearance, one must see in it the giant oak tree of happiness.

Five Reasons Why the Buddha Nature Is Taught

"All living beings have the Buddha nature"—why is this taught in Buddhism? *The Analysis of the Jeweled Nature* (Skt *Ratnagotravibhaga*)—one of the most systematic treatises on the Buddha nature concept—lists the following five reasons.

First, the Buddha nature is taught in order to encourage people to overcome their habit of "self-depreciation" (*The Uttaratantra of Maitreya*, E. Obermiller, trans., p. 238). The starting point of Buddhist practice is one's aspiration for Buddhahood—that is, one's vow to achieve a state of absolute happiness for oneself and others. All Buddhist practitioners make this vow and constantly renew it in the course of their practice. But some people—thinking that they are completely incapable of attaining Buddhahood— do not even develop such an aspiration. The Buddha nature is expounded to encourage such people to make a vow to attain absolute happiness.

Second, people may begin their Buddhist practice to cultivate their inherent Buddha nature, but some of them may think that they alone possess the Buddha nature while looking down on others, especially those who have not yet begun practicing Buddhism. To prevent such "thoughts of extreme contempt," it is taught that all people—not a select few—have the Buddha nature (ibid., 239).

Third, people are often attached to the illusion of unchanging selfhood, consumed with selfish desires, constantly thinking this or that is "mine." To help people overcome their attachment to "that which is unreal" (ibid., 239)—that is, the illusion of lesser ego—and awaken to the "true state of things" (ibid., 239)—that is, the greater self of Buddhahood—the teaching of the Buddha nature is taught.

Fourth, having learned the teaching of non-substantiality or void, some Buddhists may think that nothing is of permanent value, depreciating even the "virtuous properties that are true" (ibid., 239)—that is, the universal truth that all people possess the magnificent potential of the Buddha nature. To refute such a nihilistic view of life, the teaching of the Buddha nature is taught.

Finally, because of their selfishness, some people "cannot perceive the equality of oneself and other living beings / and become full of love for them" (ibid., 239). In order to teach the equality of all people in their capacity to attain Buddhahood and encourage mutual love and respect, the teaching of the Buddha nature is taught.

These five reasons may also be viewed as the process of awakening to the Buddha nature inherent in our lives as well as in the lives of others. To awaken to this greatest potential of life, one must challenge self-depreciation, arrogance, attachment to lesser ego, nihilism and selfishness. Put another way, challenging these delusions may be described as the very process of revealing one's Buddha nature. To deeply understand these five reasons why the Buddha nature is taught is, perhaps, to understand and manifest our inherent Buddha nature.

Freeing the Caged Bird Within

In a sense, the history of the Buddha nature concept ends with the appearance of Nichiren Buddhism, which clarifies the universally accessible method of manifesting this truth of life. Through Nichiren's teaching, however, the real history of each individual's Buddha nature begins—the baby Buddha is first discovered and nurtured, it then starts taking its toddler steps, and ultimately it grows into a strong, full-fledged Buddha inspiring many others to awaken their own sleeping baby Buddhas within.

Nichiren writes: "Myoho-renge-kyo is the Buddha nature of all living beings.... The Buddha nature that all these beings possess is called by the name Myoho-renge-kyo" (WND, 131). Regarding how to manifest one's innate Buddha nature, Nichiren explains: "When we revere Myoho-renge-kyo inherent in our own life as the object of devotion, the Buddha nature within us is summoned forth and manifested by our chanting of Nam-myoho-renge-kyo. This is what is meant by 'Buddha.' To illustrate, when a caged bird sings, birds who are flying in the sky are thereby summoned and gather around, and when the birds flying in the sky gather around, the bird in the cage strives to get out. When with our mouths we chant the Mystic Law, our Buddha nature, being summoned, will invariably emerge" (WND, 887).

In Nichiren's metaphor, our innate Buddha nature, whose name is Nam-myoho-renge-kyo, is a bird trapped in the cage of ignorance. In other words, our deluded minds create this cage that imprisons our Buddha nature. But when we chant Nam-myoho-renge-kyo to the Gohonzon, which expresses Nichiren's enlightened life and the potential of all people, our dormant Buddha nature becomes activated.

The singing of the caged bird is our chanting, and the birds flying in the sky are the Buddha nature in our environment, particularly as it is expressed in the Gohonzon. Through our chanting, the Buddha nature within our lives and the Buddha nature inherent in the universe begin their dynamic interaction.

For Nichiren's metaphor to work, however, it is necessary for the caged bird to recognize the birds in the sky as being its own kind. In other words, when we pray to the Gohonzon, rather than thinking of it as an external power or deity, we must think of it as the mirror image of our own Buddha nature. If the caged bird thinks of itself as an elephant, it is unlikely to give the slightest thought to flying.

Nichiren Buddhism clarifies that the teaching of the Buddha nature is a teaching of faith and practice. All people have it, but not many can believe in it. Furthermore, some of those who believe in their Buddha nature may not practice to manifest it, erroneously thinking—*I'm already a Buddha, so I don't have to do anything*. One's faith in the Buddha nature must be expressed in one's actions to manifest it.

Those who see the universal Buddha nature of oneself and others and work to awaken it in all people are already

Buddhas, for such actions belong to none other than a Buddha. As we cultivate our inherent Buddha nature through our conviction and actions to manifest it no matter our circumstances, we begin to see it and experience it. In our everyday lives, seeing may be believing. But in the world of Buddhism, believing in the Buddha nature is the first step toward seeing it.

(from the February 2005 *Living Buddhism*)

FOOD FOR THOUGHT:

+ How do you relate to the various metaphors of the Buddha nature discussed in this essay? What is your favorite metaphor, and why?

+ Do you sometimes feel like "I can never attain enlightenment" or "I'm already a Buddha, so I don't have to do anything"? What is wrong with these two attitudes? How does each attitude distort the teaching of the Buddha nature?

KEY POINTS FOR CHAPTER 18

1) Through his continual efforts to respect all people, Bodhisattva Never Disparaging eradicated his negative karma, purified his mind and extended his life span. He further spread Buddhism and eventually led all who had despised him to the Lotus Sutra.

2) The Nichiren Buddhist teaching of changing karma restores the original Buddhist emphasis on the role of present action changing negative karma. Furthermore, the Nichiren Buddhist concept of karma is unique because it focuses on the fundamental cause of negative karmic retribution and provides the means to change that cause.

3) The method and aim of Soka Spirit are the same as those of Never Disparaging—reconfirming people's dignity through respecting their innate Buddhahood and helping them challenge their fundamental darkness.

CHAPTER 18

Challenging Delusion, Changing Karma

THERE IS AN ELEMENT of struggle in standing for goodness. Those committed to peace fight against wars. Those committed to tolerance do not permit intolerance. Similarly, those committed to the attainment of Buddhahood for others and themselves challenge people's delusions about their innate Buddhahood. The story of Bodhisattva Never Disparaging in the Lotus Sutra shows how those committed to the bodhisattva path of altruism must challenge people's fundamental ignorance about their supreme potential.

A Man Disrespected for His Respect

An unimaginably long time ago, the Lotus Sutra says, a man bowed to everyone he met, saying: "I have profound reverence for you, I would never dare treat you with disparagement or arrogance. Why? Because you are all practicing the bodhisattva way and are certain to attain Buddhahood" (LS, 266–67). He not only believed that everyone was worthy of respect but also expressed his belief through words of praise, through his bow of obeisance. In thought, word and deed, he exemplified the central teaching of the Lotus Sutra—the universality of Buddhahood.

At that time, according to the sutra narrative, the Buddhist teaching existed in name only. In this period of the "Counterfeit Law," "monks of overbearing arrogance exercised great authority and power" (LS, 266). Held in high regard were formality rather than substance, and practitioners' status rather than action.

Monks, nuns, laymen and laywomen reacted angrily toward this man: "This ignorant monk—where does he come from, presuming to declare that he does not disparage us and bestowing on us a prediction that we will attain Buddhahood? We have no use for such vain and irresponsible predictions!" (LS, 267). Predicting one's attainment of Buddhahood was considered a matter exclusive to the realm of a Buddha's preaching. This man could not possibly do such a thing, people thought. Some even tried to beat him with sticks or threw stones at him. But he would quickly ran away and, from safety, repeat his usual words of praise in a louder voice. So, to demean him, the people gave him the name "Never Disparaging."

For many years, the man continued his practice of showing respect to everyone. He never gave up, enduring all abuse. The Lotus Sutra tells the ending of the man's story in verse as follows:

But the bodhisattva Never Disparaging
bore all this with patience.
When his offenses had been wiped out
and his life was drawing to a close,
he was able to hear this sutra
and his six faculties were purified.
Because of his transcendental powers
his life span was extended,
and for the sake of others
he preached this sutra far and wide. (LS, 270)

Through his continual efforts to respect all people, Never Disparaging eradicated his negative karma, purified his mind and extended his life span. During his prolonged life, he further spread Buddhism and eventually led all who had despised him in the past to the Lotus Sutra. The sutra also reveals that Never Disparaging was Shakyamuni in a past existence.

Changing Karma by Challenging Delusion

In the story of Bodhisattva Never Disparaging, Nichiren Daishonin sees an example of the Buddhist principle of changing karma. Nichiren writes: "Bodhisattva Never Disparaging was not abused and vilified, stoned and beaten with staves without reason. He had probably slandered the correct teaching in the past. The phrase 'when his offenses had been wiped out' indicates that, because Bodhisattva

Never Disparaging met persecution, he was able to eradicate his offenses from previous lifetimes" (WND, 199).

Here, Nichiren explains that people can "wipe out" their negative karma accumulated over many lifetimes by spreading the correct teaching of Buddhism despite their difficulties. The root cause of people's suffering, he says, lies in their opposition to the correct teaching of Buddhism; therefore, by upholding it and overcoming inevitable difficulties in spreading it, they can transform their negative karmic pattern at the deepest level.

The idea of karma predates Buddhism. When early Buddhism incorporated this ancient Indian concept, the intent was to free people from the shackles of determinism—the idea that one's destiny is fixed, in this case, by his or her past actions. Instead, early Buddhism stressed that one's present actions—not one's status, which was considered the result of past actions—determined the moral content of his or her character. Therefore, in an early Buddhist text, Shakyamuni opposes the idea that one's high status is the sign of inborn goodness: "Not by matted locks, not by clan, not by birth, does one become a brahman. In whom is truth and righteousness, he is pure and he is a brahman." (*The Word of the Doctrine: Dhammapada*, K. R. Norman, trans., p. 56).

In the course of Buddhist history, however, the early emphasis on present actions gradually shifted to an emphasis on how much negative karma one has accumulated and thus how many lifetimes it will take to expiate the moral offenses of the past. According to this view, changing one's karma becomes almost impossible; it takes an unimaginably long time. The word *karma* again became a source of despair as well as a tool for Buddhist clergy to instill fear and guilt in the minds of believers. Without showing how to change karma in the here and now, merely pointing out others' negative karma goes against the true intent of Buddhism.

The Nichiren Buddhist teaching of changing karma restores the original Buddhist emphasis on the role of present action changing negative karma. Furthermore, the Nichiren Buddhist concept of karma is unique because it focuses on the fundamental cause of negative karmic retribution and provides the concrete means to change that cause, instead of focusing on the ultimately unknowable negative causes accumulated over one's infinite past.

Nichiren writes: "The Nirvana Sutra teaches the principle of lessening one's karmic retribution. If one's heavy karma from the past is not expiated within this lifetime, one must undergo the sufferings of hell in the future, but if one experiences extreme hardship in this life [because of the Lotus Sutra], the sufferings of hell will vanish instantly. And when one dies, one will obtain the blessings of the human and heavenly worlds, as well as those of the three vehicles and the one vehicle" (WND, 199).

In this passage, Nichiren teaches that our karmic retribution can "vanish instantly" rather than us having to undergo many lifetimes of austerities. In addition, he makes it clear that eradicating our karmic retribution is in itself the "blessing of the one vehicle"—the attainment of Buddhahood.

Nichiren goes beyond the conventional Buddhist causality whereby good actions leads to enjoyment while bad actions leads to suffering. Rather, he identifies the fundamental cause of negative karma as "slander of the Law"—denial of the Lotus Sutra's essential teaching of the universality of Buddhahood. This denial ultimately stems from primordial ignorance of the fact that all people innately possess Buddhahood.

In "Letter from Sado," Nichiren writes: "My sufferings, however, are not ascribable to this causal law. In the past I despised the votaries of the Lotus Sutra. I also ridiculed the sutra itself, sometimes with exaggerated praise and other times with contempt.... This is why I have experienced the aforementioned eight kinds of sufferings. Usually these sufferings appear one at a time, on into the boundless future, but Nichiren has denounced the enemies of the Lotus Sutra so severely that all eight have descended at once.... This is what the sutra means when it states, 'It is due to the blessings obtained by protecting the Law'" (WND, 305).

Nichiren Buddhism explains that people's fundamental suffering is caused by their slander of the Law. This slander is caused, in turn, by the inability to believe in the universal existence of people's innate Buddhahood. This is called "fundamental darkness." By overcoming this delusion, we can cut the roots of our negative karma and, at the same time, reveal our innate Buddhahood. Those two aspects of the Nichiren Buddhist practice are inseparable—challenging the fundamental darkness and revealing one's innate Buddhahood.

SGI President Ikeda discusses the Nichiren Buddhist concept of changing karma as follows: "The substance of slandering the Law is disbelief; it is not believing in the existence of the Buddha nature in oneself and others. This disbelief is what fundamentally obstructs the emergence of the world of Buddhahood. It is also the root cause of various kinds of negative karma. Eradicating this disbelief and bringing forth the world of Buddhahood represent a more fundamental causality that makes it possible for us to change our karma....

"Negative karma is subsumed in the world of Buddhahood and is purified by its power. To use an analogy, the emergence of the world of Buddhahood is like the rising of the sun. When the sun dawns in the east, the stars that had shone so vividly in the night sky immediately fade into seeming nonexistence....

"Just as the light of the stars and the moon seems to vanish when the sun rises, when we bring forth the state of Buddhahood in our lives we cease to suffer negative effects for each individual past offense committed.

"In other words, this does not deny or contradict general causality. General causality remains an underlying premise of Buddhism. But it is subsumed by what might be termed a 'greater causality.' This greater causality is the causality of attaining Buddhahood. It is the causality of the Lotus Sutra and the Mystic Law" (August 2003 *Living Buddhism*, p. 47).

Nichiren and Bodhisattva Never Disparaging

Nichiren identified with Bodhisattva Never Disparaging in that both fundamentally changed their negative karma by proclaiming the universality of Buddhahood and by reversing people's ignorance of it. In "Letter from Sado," he writes: "Nichiren is like Bodhisattva Never Disparaging of old, and the people of this day are like the four categories of Buddhists who disparaged and cursed him. Though the people are different, the cause is the same" (WND, 305).

Nichiren also thought that he and Never Disparaging had three things in common: their teachings (that is, Nichiren's Nam-myoho-renge-kyo and the words of praise recited by Never Disparaging); the conditions of the time in which they propagated Buddhism (a time of religious authoritarianism and corruption); and their status as ordinary people aspiring to practice and spread Buddhism (Nichiren at the "stage of hearing the name and words of the truth" and Never Disparaging at the "initial stage of rejoicing").

In "On the Buddha's Prophecy," Nichiren writes: "[The votary of the Lotus Sutra] will [establish and] spread abroad widely throughout Jambudvipa the object of devotion of the essential teaching, or the five characters of Myoho-renge-kyo. It was the same with Bodhisattva Never Disparaging, who lived in the Middle Day of the Law of the

Buddha Awesome Sound King. He propagated widely throughout his land the teaching of twenty-four characters that begins, 'I have profound reverence for you...,' and was attacked with sticks of wood by the whole population. The twenty-four characters of Never Disparaging and the five characters of Nichiren are different in wording, but accord with the same principle. The end of the Buddha Awesome Sound King's Middle Day and the beginning of this Latter Day of the Law are exactly the same in method of conversion. Bodhisattva Never Disparaging was a practitioner at the initial stage of rejoicing; Nichiren is an ordinary practitioner at the stage of hearing the name and words of the truth" (WND, 400).

With strong confidence in the innate Buddhahood of all people, Bodhisattva Never Disparaging expressed his words of praise to everyone he met. Similarly, Nichiren and his disciples chant Nam-myoho-renge-kyo with the conviction that all people, no matter what their circumstances, can lead lives of supreme fulfillment by revealing their Buddha nature. The meaning of chanting Nam-myoho-renge-kyo is to challenge the fundamental darkness and reveal the Buddha nature, just as Never Disparaging did with his words of praise for everyone's Buddha nature.

Chanting With a Fighting Spirit

Nichiren Buddhism teaches that the essential way to change karma is to chant Nam-myoho-renge-kyo with confidence in all people's potential for Buddhahood. In *The Record of the Orally Transmitted Teachings*, Nichiren states: "This word 'belief' is a sharp sword that cuts off fundamental darkness or ignorance.... It is through the one word 'belief' that we are able to purchase the wisdom of the Buddhas of the three existences. That wisdom is Nam-myoho-renge-kyo" (p. 54).

One's deluded state of life may be compared to a world with the sun obscured by the thick layers of clouds. Without conscious efforts to remove them, the dark clouds of delusion obscure the sun of Buddhahood within. Delusion leads to unwholesome action. The negative karma thus created gives rise to suffering, and suffering further aggravates delusion. As long as the fundamental darkness remains unchallenged, one continues living in the cycle of delusion and suffering. To change one's karma means breaking this cycle.

When we chant Nam-myoho-renge-kyo with the resolve to challenge our fundamental darkness, with confidence in the existence of the sun, we can quickly remove the clouds and reveal the sun. Once the sun of Buddhahood rises in our lives, all of our karmic suffering is reduced to seeming nonexistence. With Nam-myoho-renge-kyo, Nichiren teaches, delusion is transformed into wisdom, unwholesome actions into wholesome actions, and suffering into a source of growth and genuine fulfillment. This transformation of life's causation from delusion to suffering into wisdom to joy is the meaning of changing karma in Nichiren Buddhism. The key to this fundamental change in the chain of cause and effect within our lives is chanting Nam-myoho-renge-kyo with confidence, with a fighting spirit, creating powerful winds to blow away the dark clouds of delusion and reveal the sun of Buddhahood.

Never Disparaging and Soka Spirit

The Soka Spirit movement is the SGI-USA's collective and individual efforts to challenge the distortion of Nichiren Buddhism—as seen in the Nichiren Shoshu priesthood—and encourage both self and others to awaken to life's true potential.

The method and aim of Soka Spirit are the same as those of Never Disparaging—reconfirming people's dignity through respecting their innate Buddhahood and helping them challenge their fundamental darkness. Both Soka Spirit and the actions of Never Disparaging aim to establish a humanistic religion by challenging authoritarianism, to establish respect for each person by challenging disrespect for ordinary believers perpetrated by religious authority.

While the doctrinal importance of the Lotus Sutra is found in the "Expedient Means" and "Life Span" chapters, its importance in terms of Buddhist practice lies in "Never Disparaging," the twentieth chapter. Nichiren, therefore, writes: "The heart of the Buddha's lifetime of teachings is the Lotus Sutra, and the heart of the practice of the Lotus Sutra is found in the 'Never Disparaging' chapter. What does Bodhisattva Never Disparaging's profound respect for people signify? The purpose of the appearance in this world of Shakyamuni Buddha, the lord of teachings, lies in his behavior as a human being" (WND, 851–52).

Regarding the urgency in today's world of establishing respect for all people through challenging the fundamental darkness, SGI President Ikeda writes: "The Latter Day of the Law is an age of conflict. Seemingly swept along by an irresistible force, countries and individuals are carried from one conflict to the next. The strength to stand firm against this raging current of the times can be found in an unshakable belief in the Buddha nature within ourselves and others, as well as in actions that put this belief into practice and show respect for the lives of all people. This is because the irresistible momentum that leads to conflict arises from 'ignorance' [the fundamental darkness]. In Buddhism, ignorance specifically means the lack of awareness or belief that all people possess the Buddha nature. It is also the dark impulse that drives one to disrespect human life and violate its innate dignity. The inherent devilish nature of authority and religion, the dominant cause of conflict in the Latter Day, has this ignorance as its foundation" (October 2003 *Living Buddhism*, p. 33).

Proclaiming respect for humanity in the abstract is easy, but to show sincere respect for the person confronting you is difficult—especially if the person is hostile. But this is exactly what Bodhisattva Never Disparaging did. In each person he met, he saw the Buddha nature and expressed his utmost respect through his words and behavior. His practice, at the same time, was a direct challenge to the great authority and power of arrogant monks in an age of religious corruption.

In the end, respect triumphed over disrespect, as did the Buddha nature over the fundamental darkness. Never Disparaging's negative karma gave way to the joy of living, and the name given to demean this nameless man became a name of honor in Buddhist history.

(from the September 2005 *Living Buddhism*)

FOOD FOR THOUGHT:

+ How did Bodhisattva Never Disparaging purify his mind and extend his life span? In what ways can you relate your life to the story of Never Disparaging?

+ What is the fundamental cause of negative karma according to Nichiren Buddhism? How can we change our negative karma in the here and now?

Index